# Bundt

1

Published in 2022 by Ebury Press an imprint of Ebury Publishing,
20 Vauxhall Bridge Road,
London SW1V 2SA

Ebury Press is part of the Penguin Random House group of companies
whose addresses can be found at global.penguinrandomhouse.com

Bundt ® is the registered trademark of Northland Aluminum Products, Inc. Minneapolis MN

Text © Melanie Johnson 2022
Photography © Ebury Press 2022
Design © Ebury Press 2022

Food Styling: Melanie Johnson & Bella Haycraft Mee
Food Styling Assistant: Jodie Nixon
Props Styling: Lauren Miller
Photographer: Nassima Rothacker
Image on page 252: Lilybee Gwyn-Jones
Design: Louise Evans
Production: Rebecca Jones
Publishing Director: Elizabeth Bond

This edition first published by Ebury Press in 2022

www.penguin.co.uk

A CIP catalogue record for this book is available from the British Library

ISBN  9781529195545

Printed and bound in China by C&C Offset Printing Co., Ltd.

Penguin Random House is committed to a sustainable future for our
business, our readers and our planet. This book is made from Forest
Stewardship Council® certified paper.

Melanie Johnson

# Bundt

**From everyday bakes to fabulous
celebration cakes**

EBURY
PRESS

# Dedication

For me, baking is a constant pleasure. It's a mediative escape that feeds my curiosity and desire, all the while soothing my mind. My earliest memories are of my maternal grandmother, Elfriede, preparing a magical alchemist's table in her beautiful orange grove in Australia. There were bowls piled high with mountains of sugar, cocoa powder, flour, eggs and butter melting from the scorching sun. She would leave me to experiment, free to create whatever chaos I wanted. My misshapen heap would be baked, declared a great success, and served on blue and white Meissen plates, alongside the perfectly formed, icing-sugar-dusted, chocolate and vanilla marbled Bundt my grandmother had effortlessly made.

Not so many years later, we lived in Austria, where my parents owned a fin de siècle hotel in a picturesque medieval village in the mountains. I have wonderful memories of my father, my hand held in his, as we went to visit the kitchens to watch the pastry chef prepare all the Viennese classics from Linzer torte to strudel on the vast marble tables. My mother, by contrast, was less of a foodie but generally extolled the virtues of quality, which meant that we were never short of the finest Sprungli chocolate truffles and had the most enviable kitchen garden with everything from raspberries to tayberries, marrows to beetroot, ensuring I was the queen of every school harvest festival.

The food stories flow, from my other grandmother's chocolate blancmange and my father's soufflé omelettes to my brother's perfect steak and my sister's mean schnitzel. Food was, and is, my family's language of love.

As a mother myself now, I wonder what memories will float to the surface for my daughter, Lilybee. I hope one of them will be the day we were making cupcakes and she ran away with a piping bag filled with pink cream cheese frosting. She was squeezing it into her little mouth as I chased her around the kitchen, giggling as only three-year-olds can, and in that one moment food, love, family and life were all perfectly woven together.

I like to think we all have a culinary history, unique to each of us, that encompasses a whole life of memories. So it is to my whole, wonderful, foodie family, with whom I've made so many of mine, that I dedicate this book, my true celebration of Bundt® love.

*Love Melanie x*

# *There is nothing more wonderful than baking.*

Whether it is for a celebration to be shared with family and friends or a simple slice with a cup of tea and a cozy chat, it is the comforting familiarity of making a cake that brings us all joy.

A Bundt® is often baked to share or to gift. Many of us have a deep-rooted desire to nurture through food and our Bundt® pans form the foundation of so many of these rituals worldwide.

Ever since Nordic Ware was founded as a humble kitchenware company in 1946, our focus has been to produce high-quality, innovative products designed to enrich people's lives by adding style, convenience and an extra dash of fun to baking.

Our Bundt® pans are undoubtedly our most popular product and the unique name 'Bundt' was coined by our co-founder, Dave and Dotty Dalquist, to describe the fluted design of our unique ring cake pan. This original pan, inspired by the traditional German Gugelhupf, featured a distinctive hole in the center that allowed cakes to bake evenly and from our original Anniversary design, an icon was born. Today we offer Bundt® pan designs for every celebration and season you can think of. They are used by every type of baker around the world from top chefs to home cooks. They inspire people to try new recipes, flavours and cuisines and can be used to create sweet or savoury foods.

If you want simple elegance with no complex decorating, the design and beauty is baked right into the cake when you bake with a Bundt®.

Filled with beautiful recipes, great tips and gorgeous photography, this book will show you just how versatile a Bundt® can be. We know you will return again and again to find inspiration and ideas for any occasion for years to come.

With her supreme knowledge and skill, Melanie has created a treasure trove of recipes that will become your new traditions. From easy everyday bakes to celebratory classics, there is something for everyone.

# Contents

## CHAPTER 3
# Chocolate Bundts

## CHAPTER 4
# Starstruck Bundts

# CHAPTER 5

# Swirl It Up

# CHAPTER 6

# Jelly & Ice Cream

# CHAPTER 1

# Everyday Bundts

# Classic Vanilla Bundt

––––––

Not to be underestimated, a simple vanilla Bundt is the foundation
of many a mouth-watering moment.

SERVES 8

**For the 10-cup Kugelhopf
Bundt® pan:**
15g (1 tbsp/ ½oz) butter
15g (1 tbsp/ ½oz) plain flour

**For the cake:**
250g (1 ½ cups/9oz)
   self-raising flour
250g (1 cup/9oz) golden
   caster sugar
A pinch of salt
250g (1 cup + 2 tbsp/9oz)
   unsalted butter, melted
4 eggs, lightly beaten
1 tsp vanilla bean paste
70ml (6 tbsp/2 ½fl oz)
   buttermilk

**To finish:**
Icing sugar

1. Preheat your oven to 160°C fan/180°C/350°F/gas 4.

2. Melt the butter, then use a pastry brush to brush it evenly over
   the inside of a 10-cup Kugelhopf Bundt® pan, being careful to get
   into every nook and cranny. I find it easier to brush from the base
   up to prevent any butter pooling. Sift over the flour, moving the
   pan from side to side to coat it evenly. Turn it upside down and
   give it a final tap to remove any excess, then set aside.

3. Add the flour, sugar and salt to a mixing bowl. Add the melted
   butter, eggs, vanilla and buttermilk and beat until smooth. Pour
   into the prepared pan and bake for 50–55 minutes or until the top
   is golden, the cake is coming away from the sides and a skewer
   inserted into the cake comes out clean. Leave to cool in the pan
   for 15 minutes, then invert on to a wire rack to cool completely.

4. Place on a serving plate and dust simply with icing sugar or
   choose one of the serving variations on pages 17–20. This Bundt
   will keep well in an airtight container for up to 5 days.

# Vanilla

I can't decide if vanilla is simple, or if vanilla on vanilla is actually
quite complex because with this recipe you can enjoy vanilla
entirely in its own right. The flavour is surprisingly sophisticated and
warming, especially if you use a rich vanilla paste or seeds directly
from a vanilla pod.

SERVES 8

300g (2 cups/10½oz) icing
   sugar
150g (1¼ sticks/5½oz)
   unsalted butter
2 tsp vanilla bean paste
Classic Vanilla Bundt
   (opposite page)
1 tbsp sprinkles

1. Sift the icing sugar into a bowl, add the butter and beat until
   evenly combined. Mix through the vanilla.

2. Put the buttercream into a piping bag and use it to decorate the
   Bundt or spread the buttercream over the Bundt with a palette
   knife. Scatter over the sprinkles. This Bundt will keep for 5 days
   in an airtight container.

# White Chocolate & Pistachio Vanilla Bundt

You can make your own pistachio paste by simply blitzing pistachios as you would for any nut butter and they become the most flavoursome paste, which you'll be eating by the spoonful. When I did my chef's diploma at Leith's Cookery School I was amazed by the incredible bright-green, fresh pistachios they had, which were so different to any I'd seen in any supermarket, so look out for Middle Eastern markets that sell the bright ones as they will give the best-coloured nut butter.

SERVES 8

50g (¼ cup/1¾oz) pistachio paste (see intro)
75g (½ cup/2¾oz) white chocolate
125ml (½ cup/4fl oz) double cream
Classic Vanilla Bundt (page 16)
50g (½ cup/1¾oz) pistachios, chopped

1. Melt the pistachio paste, white chocolate and cream together in a saucepan over a low heat. Pour over the Bundt and then scatter over the chopped pistachios. This Bundt will keep in an airtight container for a few days.

# Boston Cream Pie

If someone shows up with a box of doughnuts, I will always have my eye on the Boston cream one. Chocolate, vanilla pastry cream and tender, squishy vanilla cake can't help but be a match made in heaven.

SERVES 8

Classic Vanilla Bundt (page 16)

**For the filling:**
300ml (1½ cups/10fl oz) whole milk
4 egg yolks
75g (⅓ cup/2¾oz) caster sugar
15g (1 tbsp/½oz) cornflour
15g (1 tbsp/½oz) plain flour
1 tsp vanilla bean paste
175ml (¾ cup/6fl oz) double cream

**For the chocolate topping:**
100g (¾ cup/3½oz) dark chocolate
75ml (⅓ cup/2½fl oz) double cream

1. Slice the vanilla Bundt in half horizontally.

2. Put the milk in a saucepan and bring it to a simmer, without letting it boil, then remove from the heat.

3. Put the egg yolks and sugar into a bowl and whisk them together. Add the cornflour, plain flour and vanilla and whisk until smooth, then gradually add the warm milk.

4. When all the milk has been added, return the mixture to a clean saucepan. Heat over a medium heat and stir vigorously until the custard is smooth. Place in a clean bowl and cover with clingfilm so it doesn't form a skin. Chill until ready to use.

5. Softly whip the double cream, then fold it through the custard to create a crème diplomat. Use it to cover the bottom half of the Bundt. Top with the other half, lightly press it down and tidy the edges with a palette knife.

6. To make the chocolate topping, gently melt the chocolate and cream together in a small saucepan, then pour over the top of the Bundt. This will keep well in the refrigerator for a few days.

# Rosemary & Citrus Olive Oil Bundt

A deliciously damp Bundt with juicy citrus flavours and the rosemary a mere gentle whisper in the background. Serve with delicate tea and imagine you're sitting in an Italian olive grove (better still, actually be in an Italian olive grove)!

SERVES 8

**For the 10-cup Bundt® pan:**
1 tbsp olive oil

**For the cake:**
75g (1¾ cups/2¾oz) panko breadcrumbs
200g (1 cup + 2 tbsp/7oz) caster sugar
125g (⅔ cup/4½oz) ground almonds
1½ tsp baking powder
4 eggs
175ml (1 cup/6fl oz) olive oil
Zest of 1 orange
Zest of 1 lemon

**For the syrup:**
2 sprigs of rosemary
Juice of 1 orange
Juice of 1 lemon
50g (¼ cup/1¾oz) caster sugar

**To serve:**
Greek yoghurt
Sprigs of rosemary

1. Preheat your oven to 160°C fan/180°C/350°F/gas 4.

2. Brush the olive oil over the inside of a 10-cup Bundt® pan and set aside.

3. Place the breadcrumbs, caster sugar, ground almonds and baking powder in a large bowl and use a whisk to mix these dry ingredients together. In a separate bowl, whisk the eggs and oil until combined and add the citrus zests. Pour the wet ingredients into the dry and whisk again until the mixture is homogenous. Pour the batter into the prepared pan and bake for 45–50 minutes. A skewer test isn't as clear as with some cakes but it will give you an indication. Leave to cool in the pan on a wire rack so the air can circulate.

4. To make the syrup, place the rosemary, citrus juices and sugar into a small pan. Simmer over a low heat at first so the sugar dissolves, then turn up the heat to a simmer and allow to reduce and become syrupy – this will take about 5 minutes.

5. While the cake is still in the pan, use a toothpick to make holes all over it and pour over the syrup. Leave the cake to absorb the syrup. Once the cake has completely cooled, turn out onto a plate.

6. Serve with Greek yoghurt and decorate with rosemary sprigs. This cake will keep for up to a week in an airtight container and never seems to dry out.

# Snickerdoodle Bundt

If you come over for a cup of tea, chances are I'll make you this. It's a seemingly simple Bundt but that's precisely where the joy is found. Easy to make, easy to enjoy. There's something very satisfying in the simple flavour combination, and by brushing the Bundt with butter and cinnamon sugar at the end it delivers unerring comfort.

SERVES 4

**For the 6-cup Anniversary Bundt® pan:**
15g (1 tbsp/ ½oz) butter
15g (1 tbsp/ ½oz) plain flour

**For the cake:**
115g (½ cup/4oz) unsalted butter, softened
140g (¾ cup/4¾oz) golden caster sugar
2 eggs, lightly beaten
1 tsp vanilla extract
1 tsp ground cinnamon
A pinch of salt
115g (1 cup/4oz) self-raising flour
50ml (¼ cup/1¾fl oz) buttermilk

**To finish:**
50g (3 tbsp/? unsalted butter, melted
75g (5 tbsp/ ⅓ cup/2¾oz) golden caster sugar
1 tbsp ground cinnamon

1. Preheat your oven to 160°C fan/180°C/350°F/gas 4.

2. Melt the butter, then use a pastry brush to brush it evenly over the inside of a 6-cup Anniversary Bundt® pan, being careful to get into every nook and cranny. I find it easier to brush from the base up to prevent any butter pooling. Sift over the flour, moving the pan from side to side to coat it evenly. Turn it upside down and give it a final tap to remove any excess, then set aside.

3. Place the butter and sugar in a large bowl and mix with hand-held electric beaters until pale and fluffy. Add the lightly beaten eggs, one at time, mixing to combine before adding another. Add the vanilla and mix briefly to combine. Add a third of the flour and mix briefly, then add half of the buttermilk and mix. Repeat again and end with the final third of flour. Mix until just combined and smooth. Scrape the batter into the prepared pan. Bake for 25–30 minutes or until a skewer inserted into the cake comes out clean and the cake springs back to a light touch. Leave to cool in the pan on a wire rack for 10–15 minutes so the air can circulate, then invert onto the wire rack.

4. While the Bundt is still warm, use a pastry brush to brush the entire outside with melted butter. Combine the sugar and cinnamon on a plate, then roll the Bundt gently in the sugar. Sprinkle or spoon the remaining sugar over generously to cover the whole Bundt.

5. Serve warm. Store in an airtight container for up to 5 days.

# Afternoon Tea Earl Grey Bundt with Yuzu Glaze

---

This, for me, is an afternoon tea Bundt and not simply because it's scented with the floral and citrus flavours of Earl Grey tea but also because of its lightness and gentle texture. It's an easy-going cake that will get along with almost anyone. Part of Earl Grey's flavour profile is bergamot, which always sits harmoniously with other citrus flavours, including yuzu, which reminds me of grapefruit.

**SERVES 8**

**For the 10-cup Bundt® pan:**
15g (1 tbsp/ ½ oz) butter
15g (1 tbsp/ ½ oz) plain flour

**For the cake:**
200ml (1 cup/7fl oz)
    whole milk
Earl Grey tea bag
225g (1 cup/8oz) unsalted
    butter, softened
275g (1⅓ cups/9¾oz)
    caster sugar
3 eggs
1 tsp vanilla bean paste
225g (1¾ cups/8oz)
    self-raising flour
A pinch of salt

1. Place the milk in a saucepan and add the Earl Grey tea bag. Bring to a simmer, then remove from the heat and leave to infuse for 1 hour. The milk will turn brown and at this stage the flavour should be very strong and acrid but once it's in the batter it will be diluted and give a gentler undertone. Remove the tea bag.

2. Preheat your oven to 160°C fan/180°C/350°F/gas 4.

3. Melt the butter, then use a pastry brush to brush it evenly over the inside of a 10-cup Bundt® pan, being careful to get into every nook and cranny. I find it easier to brush from the base up to prevent any butter pooling. Sift over the flour, moving the pan from side to side to coat it evenly. Turn it upside down and give it a final tap to remove any excess, then set aside.

4. Place the butter and sugar in a large bowl. Mix until fluffy, then add the eggs and vanilla. Continue mixing and add one-third of the flour followed by half the infused milk, a further third of flour, the remaining milk and the final third of flour, mixing well between each addition. Pour the batter into the prepared pan and bake for 40–45 minutes or until a skewer inserted into the cake comes out clean. Leave to cool in the pan for 10 minutes, then invert onto a wire rack to cool completely.

**For the yuzu glaze:**
60ml (4 tbsp/2fl oz) yuzu juice
250g (2 cups/9oz) icing sugar,
    sifted

**To finish:**
Lemon verbena leaves

5. To make the glaze, simply pour the yuzu juice into the icing sugar and mix until smooth. Pour the glaze over the top of the cooled Bundt and scatter with the lemon verbena before serving with a cup of Earl Grey tea to really savour the delicate Earl Grey flavour. This Bundt will keep for up to 5 days in an airtight container.

# Victoria 'Bundtwich'

A Victoria sandwich is an icon of baking – historic yet deliciously simple, but I think making it as a Bundt is a genuine improvement. By baking it in a Bundt® pan you minimise the risk of any hasty rising resulting in a dipped middle, plus you have the benefit of the centre being the perfect spot for a pile of juicy summer strawberries.

SERVES 8

**For the 10-cup Swirl Bundt® pan:**
15g (1 tbsp/½oz) butter
15g (1 tbsp/½oz) plain flour

**For the cake:**
300g (1⅓ cups/10½oz) unsalted butter
200g (1 cup/7oz) caster sugar
4 eggs
1 tsp vanilla bean paste
200g (1¼ cups/7oz) self-raising flour
½ tsp baking powder
½ tsp bicarbonate of soda
A pinch of salt

**For the filling:**
200g (1 cup/7oz) fresh strawberries, halved
1 tsp vanilla bean paste
300ml (1⅓ cups/10fl oz) double cream
3 tbsp icing sugar
75g (¼ cup/2¾oz) seedless raspberry jam

**To finish:**
Icing sugar
Fresh strawberries, halved or whole, with the green stalks left on

1. Preheat your oven to 160°C fan/180°C/350°F/gas 4.

2. Melt the butter, then use a pastry brush to brush it evenly over the inside of a 10-cup Swirl Bundt® pan, being careful to get into every nook and cranny. I find it easier to brush from the base up to prevent any butter pooling. Sift over the flour, moving the pan from side to side to coat it evenly. Turn it upside down and give it a final tap to remove any excess, then set aside.

3. Place the butter and sugar in a large bowl and mix together with hand-held electric beaters until pale and fluffy. Lightly beat the eggs in a separate bowl and then add them gradually to the butter and sugar, along with the vanilla. Mix well. Add the flour, baking powder, bicarbonate of soda and salt and mix until just combined. Pour into the prepared pan and bake for 40–45 minutes or until a skewer inserted into the cake comes out clean. Leave to cool in the pan for 15 minutes, then invert on to a wire rack to cool completely.

4. Place the strawberries and vanilla in a bowl, toss to coat, and leave to macerate.

5. Whip the double cream with the icing sugar until softly whipped. Cut the Bundt in half horizontally and spread first with the raspberry jam and then pile on the whipped cream. Spoon the macerated strawberries and their juices all over the cream and then sandwich with the other half of the Bundt. Dust with icing sugar and fill the centre with fresh strawberries. Due to the whipped cream, this cake is best eaten on the day it's made.

# Lamington Bundt

---

With noble origins, lamingtons are part of Australian culture, so getting the Bundt version just right couldn't be more important. I have some really early memories of my childhood in Australia and this recipe has all of the delicious soft vanilla flavour of lamingtons smothered in their cocoa icing with the texture of sweet coconut. Lord Lamington would certainly approve.

**SERVES 8**

**For the 10-cup Bundt® pan:**
15g (1 tbsp/ ½oz) butter
15g (1 tbsp/ ½oz) plain flour

**For the cake:**
300g (2 ½ sticks/ 1 ⅓ cups/ 10 ½oz) unsalted butter, softened
200g (1 cup + 2 tbsp/ 7oz) caster sugar
4 eggs
1 tsp vanilla bean paste
200g (1 ¼ cups/ 7oz) self-raising flour
½ tsp baking powder
½ tsp bicarbonate of soda
A pinch of salt

**For the filling:**
4 tbsp raspberry jam, preferably seedless

1. Preheat your oven to 160°C fan/180°C/350°F/gas 4.

2. Melt the butter, then use a pastry brush to brush it evenly over the inside of a 10-cup Bundt® pan, being careful to get into every nook and cranny. I find it easier to brush from the base up to prevent any butter pooling. Sift over the flour, moving the pan from side to side to coat it evenly. Turn it upside down and give it a final tap to remove any excess, then set aside.

3. Place the butter and sugar in a medium bowl and cream together until pale and fluffy. Break the eggs into a small bowl and whisk them together with the vanilla. Pour this mixture gradually into the creamed butter and sugar and mix until fully combined. Sift over the flour, baking powder, bicarbonate of soda and salt, and fold until just combined. Pour the batter into the prepared pan and bake for 30 minutes or until a skewer inserted into the cake comes out clean. Leave to cool in the pan for 10–15 minutes, then invert onto a wire rack to cool completely.

4. Once cooled, slice the cake in half horizontally. Spoon the jam over the bottom half and spread it evenly, then top with the other half of the Bundt, creating a sandwich.

**For the frosting:**
200g (1½ cups/7oz)
    icing sugar
25g (¼ cup/1oz) cocoa
    powder
75g (½ cup/2¾oz) dark
    chocolate
25g (2 tbsp/1oz) unsalted
    butter
100ml (½ cup/3½fl oz)
    whole milk

**To serve:**
100g (1⅓ cups/3½oz)
    desiccated coconut
Whipped cream

5. To make the frosting, add the icing sugar and cocoa powder to a large bowl. Melt the chocolate and butter in a heatproof bowl in the microwave or over a pan of simmering water, then pour this over the icing sugar and cocoa. Whisk it in, then add the milk and continue to mix until smooth and glossy.

6. Place the Bundt on a cooling rack with a baking sheet lined with baking parchment beneath it, then pour the chocolate icing all over the Bundt. Re-use the icing caught on the parchment below to repeat this and to ensure the whole cake is covered. Sprinkle the desiccated coconut over the entire Bundt so it has an even covering all over. If you're in a warmer climate or in the summer months, chill for 30 minutes before serving.

7. Serve with whipped cream and a cup of tea. This cake will keep for up to a week in an airtight container.

# Speculoos Bundt

———

I'm not sure how anyone even came up with the idea of turning these warming little biscuits into a spread, but they deserve a prize for creating something so uniquely delicious. Whatever next? Shortbread spread? Chocolate-chip cookie spread?

SERVES 8

**For the 10-cup Bundt® pan:**
15g (1 tbsp/ ½oz) butter
15g (1 tbsp/ ½oz) plain flour

**For the cake:**
350g (1 ½ cups/12oz) unsalted
  butter, softened
250g (1 ¼ cups/9oz) soft light
  brown sugar
100g (½ cup/3 ½oz) caster
  sugar
5 eggs
350g (2¾ cups/12oz)
  self-raising flour

**For the buttercream:**
200g (7oz) Speculoos spread
  (I use Lotus)
55g (½ stick/1 ¾oz) unsalted
  butter, softened but not
  greasy
175g (1 ¼ cups/6oz) icing
  sugar
A splash of milk (optional)

**To decorate:**
8 Speculoos biscuits
  (I use Lotus Biscoff)

1. Preheat your oven to 160°C fan/180°C/350°F/gas 4.

2. Melt the butter, then use a pastry brush to brush it evenly over the inside of a 10-cup Bundt® pan, being careful to get into every nook and cranny. I find it easier to brush from the base up to prevent any butter pooling. Sift over the flour, moving the pan from side to side to coat it evenly. Turn it upside down and give it a final tap to remove any excess, then set aside.

3. Cream the butter and both sugars together in a large mixing bowl. Add the eggs, one at a time, beating between each addition, then fold through the flour until just combined. Pour the batter into the prepared pan and bake for 50–55 minutes or until a skewer inserted into the cake comes out clean. Leave to cool in the pan for 15 minutes, then invert onto a wire rack to cool completely.

4. To make the buttercream, mix the spread, butter and icing sugar together using electric beaters. If it seems a bit stiff, add a little milk to loosen it. It should be firm but spreadable.

5. To assemble, slice the Bundt in half horizontally, then either spread or pipe half the buttercream on to the bottom layer. Sandwich the top back on, then add the remaining buttercream to the top. Fill the centre with more biscuits, of course! This Bundt will keep for up to 5 days in an airtight container.

# Stickiest Ginger Bundt with Mascarpone Frosting

———

A dark, damp and dense gingery Bundt thanks to the triple load of syrups. They're all in here – black treacle, golden syrup and pomegranate molasses, and let's not forget the preserved ginger that adds the spice to that moistness. When I was testing recipes I asked my father, who is a real ginger lover, what he wanted from a ginger Bundt and he said, 'It has to be a really sticky ginger cake to get my vote and have a bit of a kick!' So, I wrapped this up in parchment, put it in a tin and he loved it.

SERVES 10

**For the 12-cup Anniversary Bundt® pan:**
15g (1 tbsp/ ½oz) butter
15g (1 tbsp/ ½oz) plain flour

**For the cake:**
225g (1 cup/8oz) unsalted butter
225g (1 cup + 2 tbsp/8oz) dark muscovado sugar
50g (4 tbsp/1¾oz) black treacle
125g (1 cup + 1 tbsp/4½oz) golden syrup
65g (5 tbsp/2¼oz) pomegranate molasses
250ml (1 cup/9fl oz) milk, either whole or semi-skimmed
350g (2¾ cups/12oz) self-raising flour
1 tsp bicarbonate of soda
1 tbsp ground ginger
1 tsp ground cinnamon
100g (1 cup/3½oz) preserved ginger in syrup, ginger chopped and syrup reserved
3 eggs, beaten

1. Preheat your oven to 160°C fan/180°C/350°F/gas 4.

2. Melt the butter, then use a pastry brush to brush it evenly over the inside of a 12-cup Anniversary Bundt® pan, being careful to get into every nook and cranny. I find it easier to brush from the base up to prevent any butter pooling. Sift over the flour, moving the pan from side to side to coat it evenly. Turn it upside down and give it a final tap to remove any excess, then set aside.

3. Put the butter, sugar, black treacle, golden syrup, pomegranate molasses and milk in a medium saucepan and gently melt them together.

4. Add the flour, bicarbonate of soda and ground ginger and cinnamon to a large bowl and use a whisk to mix them together. Add the chopped preserved ginger and beaten eggs, then pour the remaining wet ingredients over the dry. Use the whisk to mix until completely combined. Pour the batter into the prepared pan and bake for 40–45 minutes.

Ingredients and method continued overleaf →

**For the mascarpone frosting:**
225g (1 cup/8oz) mascarpone
100g (¾ cup/3½oz) icing
   sugar, sifted

**To finish:**
50g (¼ cup/1¾oz) fresh
   pomegranate seeds

5. Remove the cake from the oven and use a skewer to make holes all over the base, then brush some of the reserved ginger syrup generously over the cake. Stand the Bundt® pan on a wire rack to cool (so the air can circulate) for 10–15 minutes, then invert it onto a wire rack. While it's still warm, brush the outside of the Bundt with the remaining ginger syrup.

6. When the cake has cooled, beat the mascarpone and icing sugar together. Spoon over the Bundt, then scatter with fresh pomegranate seeds, which give a delicious tartness against the sticky sweetness of the ginger Bundt. This Bundt will remain sticky and delicious for a good few days stored in an airtight container, but it will need to be refrigerated if the mascarpone is spooned over.

# Sticky Toffee Pudding Bundt with Thick Toffee Sauce

If I'm in a restaurant and sticky toffee pudding is on the menu, then that's what I'm having. I spend many moments lamenting the fact that something quite so joyous shouldn't be consumed every day, but it does mean that when I do it has to be good. Dates can sometimes overpower the flavour, so this recipe replaces dates with dried apricots to ensure stickiness without the earthiness.

**SERVES 8**

**For the 10-cup Bundt® pan:**
15g (1 tbsp/½oz) unsalted butter
15g (1 tbsp/½oz) plain flour

**For the cake:**
200g (1 cup/7oz) dried apricots
350ml (1½ cups/12fl oz) water
300g (1¾ cups/10½oz) self-raising flour
115g (½ cup/4oz) caster sugar
175g (¾ cup + 2 tbsp/6oz) soft light brown sugar
110g (1 stick/3¾oz) unsalted butter, melted
2 tbsp black treacle
3 eggs
1 tsp vanilla bean paste
2 tbsp golden syrup

**For the toffee sauce:**
125g (1 stick + 1 tbsp/4½oz) unsalted butter
200g (1 cup/7oz) muscovado sugar
125ml (½ cup/4fl oz) single cream

**To serve:**
Double cream

1. Preheat your oven to 160°C fan/180°C/350°F/gas 4.

2. Melt the butter, then use a pastry brush to brush it evenly over the inside of a 10-cup Bundt® pan, being careful to get into every nook and cranny. I find it easier to brush from the base up to prevent any butter pooling. Sift over the flour, moving the pan from side to side to coat it evenly. Turn it upside down and give it a final tap to remove any excess, then set aside.

3. Roughly chop the dried apricots and add them to a small saucepan with the water. Bring to a simmer and then remove from the heat. Leave to sit for 10 minutes so the water becomes syrupy, then add the contents of the saucepan to a blender. Process until smooth and set aside.

4. Put the flour and sugars in a large bowl. Mix with a whisk, then pour in the apricot purée, melted butter, treacle, eggs, vanilla and golden syrup. Mix together until smooth, then pour into the prepared pan. Bake for 50–55 minutes or until a skewer inserted into the cake comes out clean. Leave to cool in the pan for 20 minutes, then turn out onto a serving plate.

5. To make the toffee sauce, put all the ingredients in a saucepan and bring to a simmer. Boil the sauce, without stirring, for a few minutes, then pour over the Bundt. Serve hot with double cream.

# Lavender Teacake Bundt with Honey Glaze & Whipped Honey Butter

This is definitely the summer garden of Bundts. It is sitting outside in the summer in dappled sunlight at a pretty table, paths lined with lavender and bumbling bees making honey, as you snip off a few sprigs of lavender to decorate your Bundt. You could infuse the milk in this recipe with fresh lavender, if you have it, but otherwise lavender flavouring does the trick.

SERVES 4

**For the 6-cup Bundt® pan:**
15g (1 tbsp/ ½oz) unsalted butter
15g (1 tbsp/ ½oz) plain flour

**For the cake:**
220g (2 sticks/ unsalted butter, softened
220g (1 cup/8oz) caster sugar
3 eggs
1 tsp vanilla bean paste
220g (1 cup/8oz) self-raising flour
About ¼ tsp lavender flavouring (quantity depends on the strength of the brand you're using)
125ml (⅔ cup/4fl oz) whole milk

**For the glaze:**
50g (¼ cup/1¾oz) honey, warmed
1 tsp boiling water

**For the whipped honey butter**
110g (1 stick/3¾oz) unsalted butter
60g (⅓ cup/2¼oz) honey
2 tbsp icing sugar

1. Preheat your oven to 160°C fan/180°C/350°F/gas 4.

2. Melt the butter, then use a pastry brush to brush it evenly over the inside of a 6-cup Bundt® pan, being careful to get into every nook and cranny. I find it easier to brush from the base up to prevent any butter pooling. Sift over the flour, moving the pan from side to side to coat it evenly. Turn it upside down and give it a final tap to remove any excess, then set aside.

3. Place the butter and sugar in a medium bowl and cream together until pale and fluffy. Break the eggs into a small bowl and whisk them together with the vanilla. Pour this mixture gradually into the creamed butter and sugar and keep mixing until fully combined. Sift over the flour and fold in until just combined. Add the lavender and taste the batter to see how strong the flavour is. It's important to keep the flavour subtle as it can become acrid if too strong. Pour the batter into the prepared pan and bake for 40–45 minutes or until a skewer inserted into the cake comes out clean. Leave to cool in the pan for 10–15 minutes and then invert on to a wire rack.

4. To make the glaze, gently warm the honey, add a teaspoon of boiling water, and then brush the warm Bundt with the honey glaze.

5. To make the honey butter, use a whisk to whip all the ingredients together until combined and smooth. Serve the Bundt warm, in delicious slices with the honey butter on the side.

CHAPTER 2

—

# Fruit
# Bundts

# Apple & Cream Cheese Pound Cake Bundt

This is such a pretty-girl-next-door kind of Bundt. With its juxtaposition of apples and cream cheese all bound together by the tenderest vanilla, it's a dependable crowd-pleaser and also happens to be both my brother's AND my mother's favourite.

SERVES 10

**For the 12-cup Anniversary Bundt® pan:**
15g (1 tbsp/ ½oz) butter
15g (1 tbsp/ ½oz) plain flour

**For the cake:**
4 large apples, peeled, cored and cut into eighths
Juice of ½ lemon
375g (1⅔ cups/13oz) unsalted butter, softened
270g (1½ cups/9¾oz) cream cheese
500g (2½ cups/1lb 2oz) golden caster sugar
6 eggs
2 tsp vanilla bean paste
A pinch of salt
400g (3 cups/14oz) self-raising flour

**To serve:**
Icing sugar, for dusting
Whipped cream

1. Preheat your oven to 160°C fan/180°C/350°F/gas 4.

2. Melt the butter, then use a pastry brush to brush it evenly over the inside of a 12-cup Anniversary Bundt® pan, being careful to get into every nook and cranny. I find it easier to brush from the base up to prevent any butter pooling. Sift over the flour, moving the pan from side to side to coat it evenly. Turn it upside down and give it a final tap to remove any excess, then set aside.

3. Gently toss the apples in the lemon juice and set aside.

4. Place the butter and cream cheese in the bowl of a stand mixer and mix until combined. Add the sugar, mix again, then add the eggs and vanilla and beat until combined. Add the salt to the flour, then spoon in gradually. Mix until you have a smooth batter.

5. Pour one-third of the batter into the prepared pan, then add the apples to the remaining batter and fold them through. Pour the remaining batter into the pan. Bake for 1 hour or until a skewer inserted into the cake comes out clean. Leave to cool in the pan on a wire rack for 10 minutes, then invert onto a serving plate.

6. Dust generously with icing sugar and serve warm with whipped cream. Store in an airtight container for up to 5 days.

# Banoffee Tres Leche (Three Milk) Bundt

---

I've never been to Mexico but eating a slice of this Mexican-inspired Tres Leche cake may just take me a step closer. It all seems so wrong to pour the three forms of milk over a freshly baked Bundt and yet it proves to be SO right! Never soggy but just a tender, squishy sponge that exudes banoffee loveliness.

SERVES 8

**For the 10-cup Bundt® pan:**
15g (1 tbsp/½oz) butter
15g (1 tbsp/½oz) plain flour

**For the cake:**
220g (2 sticks/8oz) unsalted
   butter, softened
250g (1 cup/9oz) golden
   caster sugar
3 eggs, lightly beaten
1 tsp vanilla bean paste
2 ripe bananas, mashed
220g (1 cup/8oz) self-raising
   flour
A pinch of salt

**For the 'tres leche':**
1 x 397g (1 cup/14oz)
   can condensed milk
1 x 140g (½ cup/5oz)
   can evaporated milk
100ml (½ cup/3½oz)
   whole milk

**To serve:**
300ml (1¼ cups/10½fl oz)
   whipping cream
Slices of banana
A drizzle of caramel

1. Preheat your oven to 160°C fan/180°C/350°F/gas 4.

2. Melt the butter, then use a pastry brush to brush it evenly over the inside of a 10-cup Bundt® pan, being careful to get into every nook and cranny. I find it easier to brush from the base up to prevent any butter pooling. Sift over the flour, moving the pan from side to side to coat it evenly. Turn it upside down and give it a final tap to remove any excess, then set aside.

3. Place the butter and sugar into a large bowl and mix with hand-held electric beaters until pale and fluffy. Add the lightly beaten eggs, a little at time, mixing to combine before each addition. Add the vanilla and mashed banana and mix until evenly combined. Fold through the flour and salt. Pour the batter into the prepared pan and bake for 45–50 minutes or until a skewer inserted into the cake comes out clean and the cake springs back to a light touch.

4. Remove the Bundt from the oven and prick all over with a skewer. Put the condensed milk, evaporated milk and milk into a jug and whisk together. Slowly spoon over half the 'three milks' and leave to soak for 20 minutes. Invert the Bundt onto a serving plate, make holes with a skewer again and spoon the remaining 'three milks' over the top. The cake should be tender but not soggy.

5. Whip the cream, spoon over the Bundt and add the banana slices. Drizzle over some caramel and serve. Keep refrigerated and eat within a couple of days.

# Lemon Meringue Bundt with Blueberries

Billowing meringue in all its ermine splendour will always make me happy. Anywhere it seems vaguely sensible to add meringue I think we should. It's the charming, sweet softness against the tart lemon curd in this Bundt that makes it sing and is why its namesake pie is so ubiquitous. In the name of deliciousness, I've covered the sculptural details of the Bundt, but somehow just knowing all the beauty is within is more satisfying.

SERVES 8

**For the 10-cup Chiffon Bundt® pan:**
15g (1 tbsp/ ½oz) butter
15g (1 tbsp/ ½oz) plain flour

**For the cake:**
225g (1 cup/8oz) caster sugar
Zest of 1 lemon
175g (¾ cup/6oz) unsalted butter, softened
4 eggs
1 tsp vanilla bean paste
A pinch of salt
200g (1 ¼ cups/7oz) self-raising flour
150g (½ cup/5 ½oz) lemon curd
100g (⅔ cup/3 ½oz) blueberries

**For the Swiss meringue:**
4 egg whites
250g (1 cup/8 ½oz) caster sugar
1 tsp vanilla bean paste
A pinch of salt

1. Preheat your oven to 160°C fan/180°C/350°F/gas 4.

2. Mix the sugar with the lemon zest, rubbing the zest in with your fingertips to release its fragrance.

3. Melt the butter, then use a pastry brush to brush it evenly over the inside of a 10-cup Chiffon Bundt® pan, being careful to get into every nook and cranny. I find it easier to brush from the base up to prevent any butter pooling. Sift over the flour, moving the pan from side to side to coat it evenly. Turn it upside down and give it a final tap to remove any excess, then set aside.

4. Place the butter in a large bowl and use hand-held electric beaters to mix in the lemon sugar. Add the eggs and vanilla, continuously beating, then add the salt and flour and mix until just combined. Pour half the batter into the prepared pan, then spoon the lemon curd on top. Scatter over the blueberries and cover with the remaining batter. Smooth the top and bake for 50–55 minutes or until a skewer inserted into the cake comes out clean. Leave to cool on a wire rack for 10 minutes, then invert onto the rack to cool completely.

5. To make the Swiss meringue, place all the ingredients in a heatproof bowl over a pan of simmering water, making sure the bowl does not touch the water. Whisk continuously for around 5 minutes to dissolve the sugar and heat the egg whites. Once you can no longer feel sugar grains between your fingertips (taking care not to burn yourself), or the mixture reaches 80°C (176°F) on a sugar thermometer, remove from the heat and use hand-held electric beaters or a stand mixer to whisk until the mixture is very stiff and glossy. Use a palette knife or piping bag to cover the whole Bundt in the meringue, then use a cook's blowtorch to gently brown it. This Bundt is best eaten within 2 days due to the meringue.

# Cranberry & Orange Bundt

The true delight of this Bundt is in the thin slices of orange that sit diagonally through the batter. As they cook, they not only add to the tenderness but they also impart a delightful stickiness, which is balanced by the tartness of the fresh cranberries. A real treat, particularly over the festive period.

SERVES 8

**For the 10-cup Bundt® pan:**
15g (1 tbsp/ ½oz) butter
15g (1 tbsp/ ½oz) plain flour

**For the cake:**
175g (1 ½ sticks/6oz) unsalted butter, softened
215g (1 cup/7 ½oz) caster sugar
2 oranges, zest of 1
4 eggs
1 tsp vanilla bean paste
175g (1 ¼ cups/6oz) self-raising flour
100g (¾ cup/3 ½oz) fresh cranberries, plus extra to decorate

**For the orange glaze:**
200g (1 ½ cups/7oz) icing sugar
Juice of 1 orange

**To decorate:**
Thin orange slices
Fresh cranberries

1. Preheat your oven to 160°C fan/180°C/350°F/gas 4.

2. Melt the butter, then use a pastry brush to brush it evenly over the inside of a 10-cup Bundt® pan, being careful to get into every nook and cranny. I find it easier to brush from the base up to prevent any butter pooling. Sift over the flour, moving the pan from side to side to coat it evenly. Turn it upside down and give it a final tap to remove any excess, then set aside.

3. Add the butter and sugar to a large mixing bowl and cream together until pale and fluffy. Add the orange zest, eggs and vanilla and mix again. Fold through the flour until just combined, then add the whole fresh cranberries. Pour half the batter into the prepared pan. Slice 6 as-thin-as-you-can-get-them slices of the (non-zested) orange and arrange them in the batter on an angle so they are supported by the batter but don't create a flat layer (the rind is quite deliciously marmalade-like when cooked). Pour over the remaining batter and bake for 45–50 minutes or until a skewer inserted into the cake comes out clean. Leave to cool in the pan for 15 minutes, then invert onto a wire rack to cool completely.

4. To make the glaze, simply place the icing sugar in a bowl, then squeeze over enough orange juice, little by little, until you have a pourable glaze. Pour over the Bundt, then decorate with slices of orange and fresh cranberries. This Bundt will keep well in airtight container for up to 5 days.

# Passion Fruit Crème Caramel Bundt

—————

I find crème caramel irresistible – that gentle wobble, the allure of the sweet, burnt, amber caramel. This should be deemed nursery food, and perhaps that's precisely what makes it so enchanting, and yet it's often found on the menus of Michelin-star restaurants, making it worthy of any occasion. The charm is only fortified by being baked in a Bundt® pan and then adorned with passion fruit.

SERVES 8

**For the 12-cup Bavaria Bundt® pan:**
Cake release spray (see page 240 for homemade)

**For the caramel:**
150g (¾ cup + 1 tbsp/ 5½oz) caster sugar
110ml (½ cup + 1 tbsp/ 3¾fl oz) water

**For the custard:**
250ml (1¼ cups/9fl oz) whole milk
500ml (2¼ cups/18fl oz) single cream
6 eggs
60g (4 tbsp/2¼oz) caster sugar
1 tbsp vanilla bean paste

**To serve:**
3 passion fruit
Single cream

1. Preheat your oven to 140°C fan/160°C/325°F/gas 3 and either spray a 12-cup Bavaria Bundt® pan with release spray or brush it with the homemade version, see page 240. Find a roasting tray that your Bundt® pan fits inside.

2. Place the sugar and 60ml (5 tablespoons) water into a heavy-based saucepan over a low heat. Heat until the sugar has dissolved, then increase the heat and, without stirring, simmer until a golden amber colour. Swirl the pan to distribute the colour evenly. Take off the heat and add the remaining 50ml (¼ cup/2fl oz) water – it will spit and splutter so step back, but then whisk it until smooth and pour the caramel into the prepared pan.

3. Put the milk and cream in a saucepan and heat until just simmering.

4. Add the eggs, sugar and vanilla to a mixing bowl and whisk until smooth. Gradually pour in the hot milk mixture, stirring continuously. Pass the custard through a fine-mesh sieve into the Bundt® pan. Cover snugly with kitchen foil and place it into the roasting tray in your oven. Pour boiling water into the roasting tray so that the water comes halfway up the sides of the pan, then bake for 1 hour until gently set. Remove from the oven, bring to room temperature in the pan, then refrigerate for at least 4 hours or ideally overnight, if possible.

5. To serve the crème caramel, carefully loosen the edges of the caramel with a palette knife and then invert it onto a serving plate (make sure the plate has a lip as the caramel will still be liquid). Spoon over the pulp from the passion fruit and serve with a drizzle of cream.

Image overleaf →

# Pear, Cinnamon & Almond Bundt with Salted Caramel Frosting & Sweet 'N' Salty Almonds

Sweet, juicy, squishy pears with cinnamon, ground almonds to keep it tender, and caramel offset by the salty almonds bring this Bundt together. It's a perfect afternoon treat but also fabulous for (a slightly naughty) breakfast.

**SERVES 10**

**For the 12-cup Anniversary Bundt® pan:**
15g (1 tbsp/½oz) butter
15g (1 tbsp/½oz) plain flour

**For the cake:**
340g (3 sticks/11¾oz) unsalted butter, softened
340g (1¾ cups/11¾oz) golden caster sugar
5 eggs
1 tsp vanilla bean paste
100g (⅓ cup/3½oz) Greek yoghurt
300g (1¾ cups/10½oz) self-raising flour
75g (¾ cup/2¾oz) ground almonds
A pinch of salt
1 tsp ground cinnamon
4 ripe pears, peeled, cored and cut into chunks

1. Preheat your oven to 160°C fan/180°C/350°F/gas 4.

2. Melt the butter, then use a pastry brush to brush it evenly over the inside of a 12-cup Anniversary Bundt® pan, being careful to get into every nook and cranny. I find it easier to brush from the base up to prevent any butter pooling. Sift over the flour, moving the pan from side to side to coat it evenly. Turn it upside down and give it a final tap to remove any excess, then set aside.

3. Place the butter and sugar in a large bowl and beat with hand-held electric beaters until fluffy. Add the eggs, one at a time, along with the vanilla and mix until smooth. Mix in the yoghurt. Pour over the flour, ground almonds, salt and cinnamon and mix until just combined. Gently fold through the pear pieces. Pour the batter into the prepared pan and bake for 55 minutes–1 hour or until a skewer inserted into the cake comes out clean and the cake has begun to shrink from the sides. Cool standing on a wire rack so the air can circulate for around 10 minutes, then invert onto the wire rack to cool completely before frosting.

4. Place the condensed milk, light brown sugar, butter and salt in a saucepan and bring to a simmer, mixing constantly with a small whisk. The caramel frosting will thicken as it cools, so use it when it's slightly thickened but is still pourable.

**For the frosting:**
200g (½ can/¾ cup/7oz)
  condensed milk
145g (1 cup/5¼oz) soft light
  brown sugar
60g (¼ cup/2¼oz) unsalted
  butter
A pinch of salt

**For the sweet 'n' salty
  almonds:**
100g (¾ cup/3½oz) whole
  almonds
1 tbsp honey
1 tsp sea salt
½ tsp ground cinnamon

5. Combine the almonds, honey, salt and cinnamon in a small bowl and mix so the almonds are evenly coated. Then scatter them over a baking sheet lined with baking parchment and bake for 8–10 minutes or until just browning. Set aside to cool. Once cool, roughly chop.

6. Pour the caramel frosting over the Bundt so it falls down the sides, then scatter over the roasted almonds. Store in an airtight container for a few days.

# Lychee, Raspberry & Rose Bundt

___

This is such a refreshing flavour combination and the lychee really comes
into its own the day after the Bundt is baked.

SERVES 10

**For the 10-cup Chiffon
  Bundt® pan:**
15g (1 tbsp/ ½oz) butter
15g (1 tbsp/ ½oz) plain flour

**For the cake:**
1 x 587g (1 ½ cups/1lb 5oz)
  can lychees
325g (3 sticks/11 ½oz)
  unsalted butter, softened
425g (2 ¼ cups/15oz)
  caster sugar
5 eggs
50ml (¼ cup/2fl oz)
  soured cream
325g (2 ⅔ cups/11 ½oz)
  self-raising flour
A pinch of salt
100g (1 cup/3 ½oz) fresh
  raspberries, plus extra
  to serve

**For the rose frosting:**
250g (2 sticks + 2 tbsp/9oz)
  unsalted butter
500g (3⅓ cups/1lb 2oz)
  icing sugar
10 drops of rose water
¼ tsp pink food colouring

1. Preheat your oven to 160°C fan/180°C/350°F/gas 4.

2. Melt the butter, then use a pastry brush to brush it evenly over
   the inside of a 10-cup Chiffon Bundt® pan, being careful to get
   into every nook and cranny. I find it easier to brush from the base
   up to prevent any butter pooling. Sift over the flour, moving the
   pan from side to side to coat it evenly. Turn it upside down and
   give it a final tap to remove any excess, then set aside.

3. Remove the lychees from the can and pour the syrup into a
   saucepan over a medium–high heat. Reduce the syrup by two-
   thirds. Finely dice the lychees and set aside until ready to use.

4. Place the butter and sugar into a mixing bowl and mix until fluffy.
   Add the eggs and soured cream, mix again, then fold through
   the flour and salt until just combined. Add the diced lychees and
   fold them through so that they're evenly distributed throughout
   the batter. Pour the batter into the prepared pan and then drop
   the raspberries all over the top – they will sink while baking. Bake
   for 50–55 minutes or until a skewer inserted into the cake comes
   out clean.

5. Remove from the oven and use a toothpick or skewer to make
   holes all over the Bundt, then brush the reduced lychee syrup all
   over it. Leave the Bundt to cool in the pan for about 15 minutes,
   then invert onto a wire rack to cool completely.

6. To make the frosting, put the butter and icing sugar into a large
   bowl and use hand-held electric beaters or a stand mixer fitted with
   the paddle attachment to beat until smooth. Add the rose water
   very cautiously as you need the flavour to be subtle to balance
   the lychees and raspberries. Add the pink food colouring to gently
   colour the frosting. Either use a palette knife to cover the Bundt or
   put the frosting into a piping bag fitted with a star nozzle and pipe
   roses all over the Bundt – it's easier than you might think. Serve
   with some extra raspberries on the side. This Bundt will keep for a
   few days in an airtight container and stay deliciously tender with a
   lychee flavour that really comes into its own the day after baking.

# Cherry & Almond Bundt

———

I love cherries. Especially the Italian kind that come in a rich syrup and have that marzipan-like, deep essence of heady cherry flavour only found in the best cherry pies. It's that closeness to almonds that makes them such perfect Bundt buddies in this recipe. This recipe uses these cherries and they do add sweetness, but if they're not your thing you could add fresh or even frozen cherries instead.

## SERVES 8

**For the 10-cup Bundt® pan:**
15g (1 tbsp/ ½oz) butter
15g (1 tbsp/ ½oz) plain flour

**For the cake:**
275g (2 ½ sticks/9 ¾oz) unsalted butter, softened
325g (1 ½ cups/11 ½oz) caster sugar
4 eggs
½ tsp almond extract
275g (2 ⅓ cups/9 ¾oz) plain flour, plus 2 tbsp
50g (½ cup/1 ¾oz) ground almonds
2 tsp baking powder
200g (1 cup/7oz) cherries in thick syrup, drained and syrup reserved

**For the cherry glaze:**
200g (1 ½ cups/7oz) icing sugar
120ml (½ cup/4fl oz) thick cherry syrup

**To finish:**
45g (½ cup/1 ½oz) flaked almonds
Fresh cherries

1. Preheat your oven to 160°C fan/180°C/350°F/gas 4.

2. Melt the butter, then use a pastry brush to brush it evenly over the inside of a 10-cup Bundt® pan, being careful to get into every nook and cranny. I find it easier to brush from the base up to prevent any butter pooling. Sift over the flour, moving the pan from side to side to coat it evenly. Turn it upside down and give it a final tap to remove any excess, then set aside.

3. Using hand-held electric beaters, cream the butter and sugar together in a large bowl until the mixture is pale and fluffy. Break in the eggs, one at a time, then add the almond extract and continue to beat until fully incorporated. Add the flour, ground almonds and baking powder and mix until just combined. Pour into the prepared pan.

4. Toss the cherries in the 2 tablespoons of plain flour and then spoon them over the batter. They will be enveloped by the batter as it cooks. Bake for 50–55 minutes or until a skewer inserted into the cake comes out clean. Leave to cool in the pan for 10 minutes before inverting onto a wire rack to cool completely.

5. Mix the icing sugar with the cherry syrup to form a thick paste. You may need to add a little more syrup but you want a thick, toothpaste-like consistency that will drape over the cake. Drizzle over the cake, scatter over the flaked almonds and fill the centre with whole fresh cherries. This Bundt will keep for several days in an airtight container without the fresh cherries in the centre.

# Apple Cider Doughnut Bundt

———

Close your eyes and let me transport you to an American farmers' market, where the heady smell of cinnamon and sugar is wafting through the air and apple cider doughnuts are being made. I brought a slice of that home as this Bundt is like one huge doughnut.

SERVES 10

**For the 12-cup Bundt® pan:**
15g (1 tbsp/½oz) butter
15g (1 tbsp/½oz) plain flour

**For the apples (makes 1 cup):**
300g (4 apples/10½oz)
   apples, peeled, cored and
   roughly chopped
1 tbsp golden caster sugar
½ tsp ground cinnamon
90ml (6 tbsp/scant ½ cup/
   3fl oz) water

**For the cake:**
225g (1 cup/8oz) unsalted
   butter, softened
275g (1½ cups/9¾oz)
   golden caster sugar
4 eggs, lightly beaten
1 tsp vanilla extract
135ml (¾ cup/4½fl oz)
   apple cider
225g (1¾ cups/8oz) self-
   raising flour
A pinch of salt

**To finish:**
50g (3½ tbsp/1¾oz) unsalted
   butter, melted
1 tbsp ground cinnamon
75g (⅓ cup/2¾oz) golden
   caster sugar

1. Preheat your oven to 160°C fan/180°C/350°F/gas 4.

2. Melt the butter, then use a pastry brush to brush it evenly over the inside of a 12-cup Bundt® pan, being careful to get into every nook and cranny. I find it easier to brush from the base up to prevent any butter pooling. Sift over the flour, moving the pan from side to side to coat it evenly. Turn it upside down and give it a final tap to remove any excess, then set aside.

3. Put the apple pieces into a pan and sprinkle over the sugar, cinnamon and water, then simmer gently, stirring occasionally, until entirely broken down. This will take around 15 minutes. Pour into a bowl and chill until ready to use.

4. Place the butter and sugar into a large bowl and mix with hand-held electric beaters until pale and fluffy. Add the lightly beaten eggs, a little at a time, mixing to combine before adding another batch. Add the vanilla, chilled apple sauce and apple cider and mix to combine, then add the flour and salt and mix in. Pour the batter into the prepared pan and bake for 45–50 minutes or until a skewer inserted into the cake comes out clean and the cake springs back to a light touch. Leave to cool in the pan on a wire rack for 10–15 minutes so the air can circulate, then invert on to the wire rack.

5. While the Bundt is still warm, use a pastry brush to brush the entire outside with the melted butter. Combine the cinnamon and sugar on a plate and then roll the Bundt gently in the sugar. Sprinkle or spoon the remaining sugar over generously to cover the whole Bundt. Serve warm. This will keep stored in an airtight container for a few days.

# Lemon & Courgette Bundt with Lemon Icing & Lemon Curd Whipped Cream

An everyday Bundt that feels at home in all seasons. Lemon drizzle cake is always a favourite but I rather like the addition of courgettes because they add a certain earthiness and different dimension to this classic, and let's not forget we need to eat our greens. I've also made this with gluten-free flour, which works deliciously.

SERVES 8

**For the 10-cup Heritage Bundt® pan:**
15g (1 tbsp/ ½oz) butter
15g (1 tbsp/ ½oz) plain flour

**For the cake:**
240g (1 large/1 ½ cups/8¾oz) courgette
250g (2 sticks + 2 tbsp/9oz) unsalted butter, softened
200g (1 cup/7oz) golden caster sugar
1 tsp vanilla bean paste
3 eggs
Zest of 1 lemon, plus 2 tbsp juice
200g (1 ¼ cups/7oz) self-raising flour
1 tsp baking powder
A pinch of salt

**For the lemon icing:**
60ml (4 tbsp /2fl oz) lemon juice
250g (1 cup/9oz) icing sugar

**To serve:**
300ml (1⅓ cups/10fl oz) double cream
50g (½ cup/1¾oz) lemon curd

1. Preheat your oven to 160°C fan/180°C/350°F/gas 4.

2. Melt the butter, then use a pastry brush to brush it evenly over the inside of a 10-cup Heritage Bundt® pan, being careful to get into every nook and cranny. I find it easier to brush from the base up to prevent any butter pooling. Sift over the flour, moving the pan from side to side to coat it evenly. Turn it upside down and give it a final tap to remove any excess, then set aside.

3. Coarsely grate the courgette and place it in a colander to drain any excess liquid. This step is important because without it there will be too much water in the Bundt, which will stop it from being light and fluffy.

4. Take a large bowl and beat the butter and sugar until fluffy. Add the vanilla and eggs and mix again. Add the lemon zest and juice. Squeeze any liquid out of the courgette and add to the cake batter, mixing until combined. Fold through the flour, baking powder and salt, then pour the batter into the prepared pan. Bake for 45 minutes or until a skewer inserted into the cake comes out clean. Leave to cool in the pan on a wire rack for 10–15 minutes. Once the pan is cool enough to handle, invert the Bundt onto a wire rack to cool completely.

6. Mix the lemon juice and icing sugar together with a small whisk and then pour or drizzle over the cooled Bundt.

7. When you're ready to serve, whip the double cream, then beat in the lemon curd. Serve alongside the Bundt. This Bundt will keep well in an airtight container for a few days and the pre-iced cake also freezes well for up to a month.

# Peach Melba Bundt

SERVES 8

4 peaches
75g (½ stick + 1 tbsp/2¾oz) unsalted butter, softened
75g (¼ cup/2¾oz) cream cheese
150g (1½ cups/5½oz) icing sugar, sifted
Classic Vanilla Bundt (page 16)
150g (1¼ cups/5½oz) fresh raspberries

A retro flavour combination, but that's why it's so good!

1. Take one of the peaches, remove the stone, and add the flesh to a blender to make a purée.

2. Beat the butter, cream cheese and icing sugar together and fold through the peach purée. Spread over the Bundt, then slice the remaining peaches and use to decorate. Arrange the raspberries amongst the peaches and serve. This Bundt is best eaten on the day it's made.

# Mascarpone, Strawberry & Basil Bundt

SERVES 8

150g (1½ cups/5½oz) fresh strawberries
1 tsp vanilla bean paste
75g (½ cup/2¾oz) icing sugar
200g (1 cup/7oz) mascarpone
200ml (¾ cup + 2 tbsp/7fl oz) double cream, whipped
Classic Vanilla Bundt (page 16)
A handful of fresh basil leaves, chopped

A very simple but vibrant flavour combination enhanced by the basil, which gives a hint of summer freshness.

1. Halve the strawberries and toss them in the vanilla bean paste, then leave to macerate for a few minutes.

2. Mix the icing sugar and mascarpone together, then fold through the whipped cream. Spread over the Bundt.

3. Spoon the macerated strawberries over the Bundt and decorate with the fresh basil leaves. This Bundt is best eaten on the day it's made.

# CHAPTER 3

# Chocolate Bundts

# Soured Cream Chocolate Bundt

———

This is the birthday party cake of chocolate cakes; the ultimate squishy, chocolatey, perfect-with-a-glass-of-milk, chocolate cake that you cannot get enough of. My daughter says it's the best chocolate cake she's ever eaten, so that's that!

SERVES 8

**For the 10-cup Chiffon Bundt® pan:**
15g (1 tbsp/½oz) butter
15g (1 tbsp/½oz) cocoa powder

**For the cake:**
75g (¾ cup/2¾oz) cocoa powder
300g (1½ cups/10½oz) soft light brown sugar
50g (3½ tbsp/1¾oz) unsalted butter, softened
1 tsp vanilla bean paste
235ml (1 cup/8½fl oz) boiling water
2 eggs
175ml (¾ cup/6fl oz) soured cream
200g (1¼ cups/7oz) plain flour
1 tsp baking powder
1 tsp bicarbonate of soda
A pinch of salt

1. Preheat your oven to 160°C fan/180°C/350°F/gas 4.

2. Melt the butter and then use a pastry brush to brush it evenly over the inside of a 10-cup Chiffon Bundt® pan, being careful to get into every nook and cranny. I find it easier to brush from the base up to prevent any butter pooling. Sift over the cocoa powder, moving the pan from side to side to coat it evenly. Turn it upside down and give it a final tap to remove any excess, then set aside.

3. Add the cocoa powder, sugar, butter, vanilla and boiling water to a mixing bowl and whisk until smooth and the butter has melted. Add the eggs and soured cream and mix again, then add the flour, baking powder, bicarbonate of soda and salt, whisking until you have a smooth batter. Pour the chocolate batter into the prepared pan. Bake for 45–50 minutes or until a skewer inserted into the cake comes out clean. Leave to cool in the pan for 10 minutes and then invert onto a wire rack to cool completely. This Bundt will keep in an airtight container for a few days (but I doubt it will last that long).

# Chocolate Mousse Bundt

SERVES 8

30g (2 tbsp/1oz) unsalted butter, room temperature
180g (¾ cup/6oz) cream cheese
115g (1¼ cups/4oz) icing sugar
100g (⅔ cup/3½oz) milk chocolate, plus extra to decorate
50g (¼ cup/1¾oz) dark chocolate, plus extra to decorate
225ml (1 cup/8fl oz) double cream
Soured Cream Chocolate Bundt (opposite)

Chocolate mousse is always a crowd-pleaser, so imagine it complementing the squishiest chocolate cake. Divine!

1. Mix the butter, cream cheese and icing sugar together with hand-held electric beaters. Melt the milk and dark chocolate together and then pour them onto the cream cheese mixture and mix to combine. Whip the double cream until thickly whipped and then fold it through the chocolate mixture. Refrigerate until ready to assemble and serve your Bundt.

2. Use a palette knife to spread the frosting on top of the Bundt. Make chocolate curls by dragging the back of a knife along the chocolate and sprinkle over to decorate. You could also slice the Bundt in half horizontally to add an extra layer of the mousse, if you like. Kept refrigerated, this Bundt will keep for a few days.

# Black Forest Bundt

SERVES 8

300ml (1⅓ cups/10fl oz) double cream
1 tsp vanilla bean paste
Soured Cream Chocolate Bundt (opposite)
175g (1 cup/6oz) cherries in syrup
50g (¼ cup/1¾oz) dark chocolate

Classic flavours are classic for a reason, they just work and bring joy and happiness. It's really all about the kind of cherries you use for this – I like the syrupy, too-sweet-for-some kind, but use whichever you like most.

Whip the cream and stir through the vanilla. Spread over the chocolate Bundt and top with the cherries and a generous drizzle of their syrup. Make chocolate curls by dragging the back of a knife along the chocolate. Scatter the chocolate curls over the Bundt and serve. Best eaten on the day it is made.

Image overleaf →

# Tahini Bundt

SERVES 8

120g (½ cup/4¼oz) tahini
60ml (4 tbsp/2fl oz) maple
   syrup
100ml (⅓ cup + 2 tbsp/
   3½fl oz) double cream
A pinch of salt
Soured Cream Chocolate
   Bundt (page 58)
75g (½ cup/2¾oz) sesame
   halwa

Tahini has really made its mark in baking. It is for good reason as it has a depth of earthiness that sits comfortably with chocolate and seems to make everything just that little bit more lovely. You could also whisk it through Greek yoghurt and add a dollop of that alongside when serving, to double up the tahini factor.

Heat the tahini, maple syrup and cream together in a pan over a low heat and add the salt. Pour over the Bundt and crumble over pieces of sesame halwa. This Bundt will keep for a few days in an airtight container.

# Almost Affogato Bundt

SERVES 8

100g (¾ cup/3½oz) dark
   chocolate
75ml (⅓ cup/2½fl oz) strong
   espresso shot
230ml (1 cup/8fl oz) double
   cream
Soured Cream Chocolate
   Bundt (page 58)
Small tub of vanilla ice cream

I love this Bundt for sharing with friends. Serve at the table with scoops of vanilla ice cream piled in the centre and then pour the coffee sauce over the Bundt at the table for a little drama.

1. Gently melt the chocolate, coffee and cream together in a small saucepan. Scoop balls of vanilla ice cream into the centre of the Bundt and then pour the chocolate sauce all over it.

2. This bundt won't keep beyond dinner if you fill the centre with ice cream but you can also serve it sliced with ice cream on the side with the sauce poured over individual plates.

# Rich Double Chocolate Bundt
# with Caramel

This is for those days when nothing but chocolate cake will do – when you're looking for a decadent hit for the senses. It's at its best served warm with a voluptuous embrace of hot caramel, when it's also perfect for a dinner party, if there is any left it will stay tender for a good few days to snack on, too.

SERVES 8

**For the 10-cup Bavaria Bundt® pan:**
15g (1 tbsp/ ½oz) butter
15g (1 tbsp/ ½oz) cocoa powder

**For the cake:**
280g (2 ½ sticks/ 10oz) unsalted butter, softened
150g (¾ cup/5 ¼oz) soft light brown sugar
150g (¾ cup/5 ¼oz) golden caster sugar
1 tsp vanilla bean paste
A pinch of salt
5 large eggs
125g (1 ¼ cups/4 ½oz) cocoa powder
125ml (¼ cup/4fl oz) boiling water
175g (1 ¼ cups/6oz) self-raising flour
175g (1 cup/6oz) dark chocolate chips

**For the caramel:**
125g (1 stick + 1 tbsp/4 ½oz) unsalted butter
200g (1 cup/7oz) dark muscovado sugar
125ml (½ cup/4fl oz) double cream

1. Preheat your oven to 160°C fan/180°C/350°F/gas 4.

2. Melt the butter, then use a pastry brush to brush it generously over the inside of a 10-cup Bavaria Bundt® pan, being careful to get into every nook and cranny. I find it easier to brush from the base up to prevent any butter pooling. Sift over the cocoa powder, moving the pan from side to side to coat it evenly, then tap it while inverted to remove any excess cocoa. Set aside until ready to use.

3. To a large mixing bowl, add the softened butter and beat until smooth. Pour in both sugars and then mix again until fully combined and an even golden colour. Add the vanilla, salt and eggs and mix again until smooth and mousse-like. Make a paste from the cocoa powder and boiling water in a separate bowl and then pour it over the cake batter. Mix again, then fold through the flour and chocolate chips. Pour the batter into the prepared pan and bake for 45–50 minutes or until a skewer inserted into the cake comes out clean. Leave to cool in the pan for 10 minutes, so it holds its shape and releases in one piece, then invert onto a wire rack.

4. To make the caramel, add the butter, sugar and double cream to a small saucepan and bring to a simmer. Remove from the heat and pour all over the Bundt.

5. Serve the Bundt warm, covered in the caramel, with vanilla ice cream on the side. Store in an airtight container, ideally with the caramel kept separately in the fridge.

# Peanut Butter Cup Bundt

When I was little, my neighbour and best friend, Beth, was an American from Iowa. To me that was the coolest thing imaginable and she introduced me to Tootsie Rolls, Lucky Charms and Reese's peanut butter cups. At that time my mother had to take me to the American shop if I wanted to have my own, but now they're available everywhere. Chocolate with peanut butter is a flavour combination that has stayed with me.

SERVES 8

300ml (1⅓ cups/10fl oz) double cream
75g (½ cup/2¾oz) icing sugar
180g (¾ cup/6oz) smooth peanut butter
1 tsp vanilla bean paste
A pinch of salt
Soured Cream Chocolate Bundt (page 58)
100g (1 cup/3½oz) mini peanut butter cups, or 50g (¼ cup + 1tbsp) peanuts to decorate

1. Whip the double cream and then add the icing sugar, peanut butter, vanilla and salt. Beat everything together until smooth, then spoon over the Bundt.

2. Decorate with chopped mini peanut butter cups or roughly chopped peanuts. This Bundt will keep for several days in an airtight container.

# Chocolate & Almond Olive Oil Bundt

───────

This is a grown-up chocolate Bundt. It's for the day your elegant Italian friend is popping over for a coffee and she arrives looking super chic but thinks you're so clever for making such a fabulous cake.

SERVES 8

**For the 10-cup Bundt® pan:**
15g (1 tbsp/½oz) butter
15g (1 tbsp/½oz) cocoa powder

**For the cake:**
100g (½ cup/3½oz) dark chocolate
30g (2 tbsp/1oz) cocoa powder
50ml (¼ cup/2fl oz) boiling water
50g (½ cup/1¾oz) ground almonds
150g (¾ cup/5½oz) golden caster sugar
75g (⅓ cup/2¾oz) soft light brown sugar
200g (1¼ cups/7oz) self-raising flour
1 tsp sea salt
175ml (1 cup /6fl oz) extra virgin olive oil
4 eggs
75g (⅓ cup/2¾oz) mascarpone
1 tsp vanilla bean paste

**For the frosting:**
25g (2 tbsp/1oz) cocoa powder
200g (1½ cups/7oz) icing sugar
4 tbsp milk, or more to loosen
1 tsp vanilla bean paste

1. Preheat your oven to 160°C fan/180°C/350°F/gas 4.

2. Melt the butter, then use a pastry brush to brush it evenly over the inside of a 10-cup Bundt® pan, being careful to get into every nook and cranny. I find it easier to brush from the base up to prevent any butter pooling. Sift over the cocoa powder, moving the pan from side to side to coat it evenly. Turn it upside down and give it a final tap to remove any excess, then set aside.

3. Melt the chocolate and set aside to cool.

4. Make a paste with the cocoa powder and boiling water and set aside to cool.

5. Add the ground almonds, both sugars, flour and salt to a large mixing bowl. In a separate bowl, whisk together the olive oil, eggs, mascarpone and vanilla. Pour this mixture over the dry ingredients, mix, then add the melted chocolate and cocoa paste. Beat until smooth. Pour the batter into the prepared pan and bake for 40–45 minutes. Leave to cool in the pan for 15 minutes, then invert onto a wire rack to cool completely.

6. Place the cocoa powder and icing sugar in a bowl and add the milk and vanilla. Whisk until smooth – adding a little more milk if needed – and then pour over the Bundt. Scatter over the flaked almonds and serve. This Bundt will keep for a few days in an airtight container.

───────

**To decorate:**
50g (⅔ cup/1¾oz) flaked almonds, lightly toasted

# Chocolate Bundt with Mint Frosting

I've always loved an after dinner mint, smart ones with the ceremony of a proud box and gold lettering, supermarket ones with their more viscous centres – all of them. You could say I'm an After Dinner Mintaholic. I have a sentimental preference for the ones that are wrapped in gold foil but only because as a child my father would shape them into fairy sized wine goblets that I could then clink between imaginary friends as my parents continued their dinner party.

It was that feeling that inspired this recipe, the joyous rustle of people in your home, everyone lingering at the table after dinner. To bite into this dark, damp chocolate cake, smothered in a refreshingly soft mint frosting is such a simple pleasure but the Kugelhopf Bundt® tin and the delicate but easy-to-make mint leaves bring a true feeling of celebration for all seasons.

SERVES 8

**For the 10-cup Kugelhopf Bundt® pan:**
15g (1 tbsp/½oz) butter
15g (1 tbsp/½oz) cocoa powder

**For the cake:**
75g (¾ cup/2¾oz) cocoa powder
300g (1½ cups/10½oz) golden caster sugar
50g (3½ tbsp/1¾oz) unsalted butter
1 tsp vanilla bean paste
235ml (1 cup/8½fl oz) boiling water
2 eggs
175g (¾ cup/6oz) Greek yoghurt
200g (1¼ cups/7oz) plain flour
1 tsp baking powder
1 tsp bicarbonate of soda
A pinch of salt

1. Preheat your oven to 160°C fan/180°C/350°F/gas 4.

2. Melt the butter, then use a pastry brush to brush it evenly over the inside of a 10-cup Kugelhopf Bundt® pan, being careful to get into every nook and cranny. I find it easier to brush from the base up to prevent any butter pooling. Sift over the cocoa powder, moving the pan from side to side to coat it evenly. Turn it upside down and give it a final tap to remove any excess, then set aside.

3. Add the cocoa powder, caster sugar, butter, vanilla and boiling water to a mixing bowl and whisk until smooth and the butter has melted and the sugar dissolved.

4. In a separate small bowl, whisk together the eggs and yoghurt.

5. Add the flour, baking powder, bicarbonate of soda and salt to a large mixing bowl. Use a whisk to combine, then pour over the eggs and yoghurt and chocolate mixtures and mix with a whisk until you have a smooth batter. Pour the batter into the prepared pan and bake for 40–45 minutes or until a skewer inserted into the cake comes out clean. Leave to cool in the pan on a wire rack for 10 minutes and then invert onto the wire rack to cool completely.

Ingredients and method continued overleaf →

**For the mint frosting:**
50g (3 ½ tbsp/1 ¾oz) butter
150g (1 ½ cups/5 ½oz) icing
  sugar
65ml (4 tbsp) single cream
1 ¼ tsp mint flavouring

**To decorate:**
Edible silver balls
Dark chocolate, melted
12 fresh mint leaves
Mint chocolates

6. To make the mint frosting, simply add all the ingredients to a mixing bowl, if using electric beaters, or the bowl of a stand mixer, and mix until smooth.

7. Once the cake is completely cool, pipe or spread the mint frosting on to the Bundt and then decorate with silver balls, chocolate leaves (simply brush melted chocolate on to mint leaves, allow to set and then peel the leaf back) and mint chocolates. Serve with fresh mint tea and store in an airtight container for a few days.

# Chocolate Violet Cream Bundt with Blackberries

This will always remind me of my English grandmother. She wasn't much of a cook so don't be under any illusions this is 'granny's recipe' but I love the idea of time travelling through food. In a hundred years they'll probably look back on us and see everything was all about chocolate, caramel and tahini, but for my grandmother's generation it was all about violet and rose creams. Be sure to use these as subtle flavours, though, otherwise you end up with bar of soap.

**For the 10-cup Blossom
    Bundt® pan:**
15g (1 tbsp/ ½oz) butter
15g (1 tbsp/ ½oz) plain flour

**For the cake:**
250g (2 cups/9oz) self-raising
    flour
400g (2 cups/14oz) golden
    caster sugar
75g (½ cup+3 tbsp/2¾oz)
    cocoa powder
2 tsp baking powder
½ tsp salt
3 eggs
200ml (1 cup/7fl oz) buttermilk
120g (¾ cup/4¼oz) unsalted
    butter, melted
2 tsp vanilla bean paste
100ml (½ cup/3½fl oz) boiling
    instant coffee
150g (1 cup + 1 tbsp/5½oz)
    fresh blackberries, plus extra
    to decorate

**For the frosting:**
75g (⅓ cup/2¾oz) unsalted
    butter, softened
75g (⅓ cup/2¾oz) cream
    cheese
150g (1 cup/5½oz) icing sugar,
    sifted
1 tsp violet syrup (test as you
    go as you want the flavour
    to be subtle)

**To decorate:**
12 fresh blackberries
Sugared or fresh violet flowers
    (optional)
Milk and white chocolate curls
    (optional)

1. Preheat your oven to 160°C fan/180°C/350°F/gas 4.

2. Melt the butter, then use a pastry brush to brush it evenly over
   the inside of a 10-cup Blossom Bundt® pan, being careful to get
   into every nook and cranny. I find it easier to brush from the base
   up to prevent any butter pooling. Sift over the flour, moving the
   pan from side to side to coat it evenly. Turn it upside down and
   give it a final tap to remove any excess, then set aside.

3. Take a large bowl and add the flour, sugar, cocoa powder, baking
   powder and salt. Using hand-held electric beaters, slowly mix
   the dry ingredients together. Make a well in the centre and then
   add the eggs, buttermilk, melted butter, vanilla and coffee. Mix
   until smooth. Pour into the prepared pan and then drop the
   blackberries on top – they'll sink through while cooking. Bake for
   50–55 minutes or until a skewer inserted into the cake comes
   out clean. Leave to cool in the pan for 15 minutes and then invert
   onto a wire rack to cool completely.

4. To make the frosting, beat the butter, cream cheese and icing
   sugar together. Pour in the violet syrup a little at a time and taste
   test it. Different brands of syrup vary in strength, so make sure
   the flavour is very subtle. Add the splash of milk, if needed to
   loosen it. Frost the Bundt using a palette knife or transfer the
   frosting to a piping bag and pipe it over.

5. Decorate the top with blackberries, violet flowers or chocolate
   curls.

# Cookies 'n' Cream Bundt

This is by far my most requested Bundt. 'It's my birthday will you make the cookies 'n' cream Bundt?' 'My friend is coming will you make the cookies 'n' cream Bundt?' 'I really need chocolate, pleeeaaase make the cookies 'n' cream Bundt!' So I showed my daughter how to make it herself!

SERVES 10

**For the 10-cup Chiffon Bundt® pan:**

15g (1 tbsp/ ½oz) butter
15g (1 tbsp/ ½oz) plain flour

**For the cake:**

75g (¾ cup/2¾oz) cocoa powder
300g (1 ½ cups/10 ½oz) soft light brown sugar
50g (3 ½ tbsp/1 ¾oz) unsalted butter, softened
1 tsp vanilla bean paste
235ml (1 cup/8 ½fl oz) boiling water
2 eggs
175ml (¾ cups/6fl oz) buttermilk
200g (1 ¼ cups/7oz) plain flour
1 tsp baking powder
1 tsp bicarbonate of soda
A pinch of salt
6 chocolate sandwich cookies
240g (1 ¼ cups/8 ½oz) cream cheese

**For the frosting:**

45g (3 tbsp/1 ½oz) unsalted butter, softened
75g (⅓ cup/2¾oz) cream cheese
400g (3 cups/14oz) icing sugar
1 tbsp whole milk, if needed
3 chocolate and vanilla sandwich cookies, crushed

1. Preheat your oven to 160°C fan/180°C/350°F/gas 4.

2. Melt the butter, then use a pastry brush to brush it evenly over the inside of a 10-cup Chiffon Bundt® pan, being careful to get into every nook and cranny. I find it easier to brush from the base up to prevent any butter pooling. Sift over the flour, moving the pan from side to side to coat it evenly. Turn it upside down and give it a final tap to remove any excess, then set aside.

3. Add the cocoa powder, sugar, butter, vanilla and boiling water to a mixing bowl and whisk until smooth and the butter has melted. Add the eggs and buttermilk, mix again, followed by the flour, baking powder, bicarbonate of soda and salt, whisking until you have a smooth batter. Pour the chocolate batter into the prepared pan. Take the chocolate sandwich cookies and split them open. Divide the cream cheese evenly between each one to create chubby sandwiches. Drop the sandwiches on to the batter and spread evenly – they will be swallowed by the batter when cooking. Bake for 45–50 minutes or until a skewer inserted into the cake comes out clean. Leave to cool in the pan for 10 minutes and then invert onto a wire rack to cool completely.

4. To make the frosting, beat the butter, cream cheese and icing sugar together until smooth. Add the milk if needed to loosen and then fold through the crushed cookies. Use a palette knife or piping bag to frost the Bundt the way you like it. Decorate with more cookies and serve. This Bundt will keep for a day in an airtight container but best to refrigerate if needed for any longer due to the cream cheese frosting.

**To decorate:**

Chocolate and vanilla sandwich cookies

# Vegan Chocolate & Coconut Bundt with Coconut Caramel

Vegan cakes can sometimes reinforce my love of butter, so I've created a really delicious Bundt that could be appreciated on its own merit, rather than for its omission of anything. The high cocoa content and the coconut works so sublimely together that this easy, one-bowl recipe should simply be called a 'chocolate and coconut Bundt' as the fact that it's vegan is mere coincidence.

SERVES 8

**For the 10-cup Bavaria Bundt® pan:**
45g (3 tbsp/1½oz) coconut oil
45g (3 tbsp/1½oz) cocoa powder

**For the cake:**
325g (2½ cups/11½oz) self-raising flour
85g (⅔ cup/3oz) cocoa powder
325ml (1⅓ cups/12fl oz) coconut milk drink (not from a can)
275g (1¼ cups/9¾oz) soft light brown sugar
125g (½ cup/4½oz) virgin cold-pressed coconut oil
1 tbsp apple cider vinegar
1 tsp vanilla bean paste
½ tsp baking powder
½ tsp bicarbonate of soda
125ml (⅔ cup/4fl oz) sparkling water

**For the coconut caramel:**
160ml (⅔ cup/5½fl oz) coconut cream
1 tbsp virgin cold-pressed coconut oil
340g (1½ cups/11¾oz) soft light brown sugar
1 tsp vanilla bean paste
1 tsp sea salt

1. Preheat your oven to 160°C fan/180°C/350°F/gas 4.

2. Melt the coconut oil, then use a pastry brush to brush it generously over the inside of a 10-cup Bavaria Bundt® pan, being careful to get into every nook and cranny. I find it easier to brush from the base up to prevent any oil pooling. Sift over the cocoa powder, moving the pan from side to side to coat it evenly, then tap it while inverted to remove any excess cocoa. Set aside until ready to use.

3. Add the flour, cocoa powder, coconut milk, sugar, oil, vinegar, vanilla, baking powder, bicarbonate of soda and sparkling water to a mixing bowl. Beat until smooth – using hand-held electric beaters is the easiest way to do this. Pour the batter into the prepared pan and bake for 50–55 minutes or until a skewer inserted into the cake comes out clean. Leave to cool in the pan for 15 minutes and then invert onto a wire rack.

4. To make the coconut caramel, place the coconut cream, oil, sugar, vanilla and salt in a small saucepan and heat until simmering. Use a whisk to combine everything evenly.

5. I like this Bundt served warm, drizzled with caramel and topped with coconut rather like an alternative sticky toffee pudding. This Bundt will keep for a few days in an airtight container.

**To decorate:**
2 tbsp dried coconut flakes or chips (optional)

# Hot Chocolate Bundt
# with Marshmallows

Are you feeling cosy? I'm picturing Fair Isle jumpers, snow falling outside, you open the door, take your snowy boots off and find an irresistible hot chocolate Bundt with hot chocolate sauce, filled with marshmallows waiting for you. The hot chocolate sauce is quite possibly the most indulgent hot chocolate you have ever had, but baby it's cold outside.

SERVES 8

**For the 10-cup Bundt® pan:**
15g (1 tbsp/½oz) butter
15g (1 tbsp/½oz) cocoa powder

**For the cake:**
250g (2 cups/9oz) self-raising flour
400g (2 cups/14oz) soft light brown sugar
100g (1 cup/3½oz) cocoa powder
A pinch of salt
1 tsp vanilla bean paste
110g (1 stick/3¾oz) unsalted butter, melted
4 eggs, lightly beaten
240ml (1 cup/8½fl oz) soured cream

**For the hot chocolate sauce:**
225ml (1 cup/8fl oz) double cream
25g (2 tbsp/1oz) unsalted butter
30g (2 tbsp/1oz) cocoa powder
30g (2 tbsp/1oz) caster sugar
75g (5 tbsp/2¾oz) dark or milk chocolate, broken into pieces

**To finish:**
150g (2 cups/5½oz) large marshmallows

1. Preheat your oven to 160°C fan/180°C/350°F/gas 4.

2. Melt the butter, then use a pastry brush to brush it evenly over the inside of a 10-cup Bundt® pan, being careful to get into every nook and cranny. I find it easier to brush from the base up to prevent any butter pooling. Sift over the cocoa powder, moving the pan from side to side to coat it evenly. Turn it upside down and give it a final tap to remove any excess, then set aside.

3. Place the flour, sugar, salt and cocoa powder in a large bowl and use a whisk to mix them together. Pour over the vanilla, melted butter, eggs and soured cream. Whisk the mixture together and pour into the prepared pan. Bake for 45 minutes or until a skewer inserted into the cake comes out clean and you see the edges pulling away from the sides of the pan. Leave to cool in the pan for 10 minutes and then invert onto a serving plate (make sure the plate has a lip or the sauce will go everywhere).

4. To make the hot chocolate sauce, add the double cream, butter, cocoa powder and sugar to a small saucepan. Heat gently and whisk until smooth and almost boiling but make sure it doesn't actually boil. Remove from the heat and drop in the chocolate pieces. Stir until the chocolate has melted.

5. Pour the hot chocolate sauce all over the Bundt. Pile the centre of the Bundt high with marshmallows and serve hot. It will, of course, also work plated individually by the slice, drizzled with hot chocolate sauce and with a few marshmallows on the side. This Bundt will keep in an airtight container for several days and the chocolate sauce is best stored in the refrigerator and heated when needed.

# Banana & Chocolate Chip Bundt with a Maple & Sea Salt Crust

For this particular recipe I learned that sometimes more really is more. I made the same Bundt a few times with different amounts of chocolate chips and there was a resounding 'we like the one with more chocolate' from everyone (well, my four nieces and their friends). The large number of chocolate chips makes this a truly banana AND chocolate experience but it's actually the simple maple syrup and sea salt crust that takes it to a whole new level. This is my sister's current favourite (although she changes her mind nearly every time I bake).

**SERVES 10**

**For the 12-cup Anniversary Bundt® pan:**
15g (1 tbsp/½oz) butter
15g (1 tbsp/½oz) plain flour

**For the cake:**
225ml (1½ cups/8fl oz) vegetable oil
225g (1¾ cups/8oz) light muscovado sugar
1 tsp vanilla bean paste
3 eggs
3 overripe bananas, roughly 350g (1½ cups/12oz), mashed
1 tsp ground cinnamon
1 tsp baking powder
1 tsp bicarbonate soda
225g (1¾ cups/8oz) self-raising flour
340g (2 cups/11¾oz) bittersweet and semisweet chocolate chips
125g (1 cup/4½oz) chopped walnuts (optional)

1. Preheat your oven to 160°C fan/180°C/350°F/gas 4.

2. Melt the butter, then use a pastry brush to brush it evenly over the inside of a 12-cup Anniversary Bundt® pan, being careful to get into every nook and cranny. I find it easier to brush from the base up to prevent any butter pooling. Sift over the flour, moving the pan from side to side to coat it evenly. Turn it upside down and give it a final tap to remove any excess, then set aside.

3. Add the oil, sugar, vanilla, eggs and mashed bananas to a large bowl. Mix well with a whisk or hand-held electric beaters until combined. Pour in the cinnamon, baking powder, bicarbonate of soda and flour and fold it through. Once combined, add the chocolate chips and walnuts (if using), stir through, then pour into the prepared pan. Bake for 50–55 minutes or until a skewer inserted into the cake comes out clean. Leave to cool in the pan on a wire rack for 10 minutes and then invert onto the wire rack.

4. While the cake is still warm, whisk the maple syrup and bourbon (if using) together and brush all over the Bundt. Sprinkle over the sea salt. This tastes delicious served warm with chocolate ice cream and will remain tender for up to 5 days stored in an airtight container.

**To finish:**
70ml (¼ cup/2½fl oz) maple syrup
3 tbsp bourbon (optional)
1 tsp sea salt flakes

# CHAPTER 4

# Starstruck Bundts

# Hummingbird Bundt

Has a cake ever had a more romantic name? Red velvet is certainly in the running but 'hummingbird' conjures images of brightly coloured birds with a tropical backdrop of palm trees and turquoise water. The name has done its job, pineapple and coconut will take you to the island of Jamaica, where the hummingbird cake originated in the 1960s.

SERVES 8

**For the 10-cup Swirl Bundt® pan:**
15g (1 tbsp/ ½oz) butter
15g (1 tbsp/ ½oz) plain flour

**For the cake:**
225g (1 cup/8oz) unsalted butter, melted
200g (1 cup + 2 tbsp/7oz) golden caster sugar
3 eggs, beaten
1 tbsp vanilla bean paste
225g (2 large bananas/8oz) bananas, mashed
200g (1 cup/7oz) canned crushed pineapple
65g (¾ cup/2¼oz) desiccated coconut
225g (1¾ cups/8oz) self-raising flour
100g (1 cup/3½oz) pecans and walnuts, chopped

**For the cream cheese frosting:**
1 tsp vanilla bean paste
125g (¾ cup/4½oz) cream cheese
50g (3½ tbsp/1¾oz) unsalted butter, softened
300g (2¾ cups/10½oz) icing sugar, sifted
50ml single cream, or more to loosen

**To decorate:**
2 passion fruit

1. Preheat your oven to 160°C fan/180°C/350°F/gas 4.

2. Melt the butter, then use a pastry brush to brush it evenly over the inside of a 10-cup Swirl Bundt® pan, being careful to get into every nook and cranny. I find it easier to brush from the base up to prevent any butter pooling. Sift over the flour, moving the pan from side to side to coat it evenly. Turn it upside down and give it a final tap to remove any excess, then set aside.

3. Add the melted butter and sugar to a bowl and whisk together. Add the eggs and beat until smooth, then add the vanilla, mashed bananas and pineapple, mixing until homogenous. Add the coconut and flour and fold them through, followed by the pecans and walnuts. Pour into the prepared pan and bake for 45–50 minutes or until a skewer inserted into the cake comes out clean. Leave to cool in the pan for 15 minutes before turning out onto a wire rack to cool completely.

4. To make the frosting, combine the cream cheese, vanilla and butter in the bowl of a stand mixer (or use hand-held electric beaters) and then gradually add the icing sugar. Pour the cream in and mix again until you have a thick but pourable frosting.

5. Spread the frosting evenly over the Bundt, sprinkle over desiccated coconut and briefly leave to set. Just before serving, slice the passion fruit in half and spoon the pulp over the top. You could serve fresh pineapple on the side and use the pineapple crown to decorate the centre too, if you like. Serve with tropical pride! This Bundt keeps well in an airtight container for several days.

# S'mores Bundt

Inspired by the unassuming fireside snack, this Bundt was always going to be a winner. Its three simple elements of chocolate, marshmallow and biscuit satisfy any demand for indulgence. Did someone say they wanted s'more?

**SERVES 12**

**For the 12-cup Anniversary Bundt® pan:**
15g (1 tbsp / ½oz) butter
15g (1 tbsp / ½oz) cocoa powder

**For the cake:**
75g (⅓ cup / 1¾oz) cocoa powder
135g (1 cup / 4¾oz) soft light brown sugar
175g (1 cup / 6oz) golden caster sugar
50g (3½ tbsp / 1¾oz) unsalted butter
1 tsp vanilla bean paste
235ml (1 cup / 8½fl oz) boiling water
2 eggs
175ml (¾ cup / 6fl oz) soured cream
200g (1½ cups / 7oz) plain flour
A pinch of salt
1 tsp baking powder
½ tsp bicarbonate of soda
8 digestive biscuits

1. Preheat your oven to 160°C fan/180°C/350°F/gas 4.

2. Melt the butter, then use a pastry brush to brush it evenly over the inside of a 12-cup Anniversary Bundt® pan, being careful to get into every nook and cranny. I find it easier to brush from the base up to prevent any butter pooling. Sift over the cocoa powder, moving the pan from side to side to coat it evenly. Turn it upside down and give it a final tap to remove any excess, then set aside.

3. Take a large mixing bowl and add the cocoa powder, both sugars, butter and vanilla. Pour over the boiling water and then use a whisk to mix everything together until smooth. Whisk the eggs and soured cream together in a small bowl and then mix them into the chocolate mixture. Fold through the flour, salt, baking powder and bicarbonate of soda.

4. Pour half the mixture into the prepared pan, then arrange the digestive biscuits in a single, flat layer over the batter. Pour the remaining batter over the top and then bake for 40–45 minutes. Leave to cool in the pan for 15 minutes and then invert onto a wire rack to cool completely.

**For the marshmallow fluff frosting:**
4 egg whites
300g (1¾ cups/3¾oz) caster sugar
A pinch of salt
1 tsp vanilla bean paste

5. Once the Bundt is completely cool, make the marshmallow frosting. Put the egg whites, sugar and salt into the bowl of a stand mixer. Bring a pan of a few inches of water to the boil and then stand the bowl on top of the pan. Whisk continuously for around 5 minutes to dissolve the sugar and heat the egg whites. Once you can no longer feel sugar grains between your fingertips (taking care not to burn yourself), or the mixture reaches 80°C (176°F) on a sugar thermometer, remove from the heat and use hand-held electric beaters or a stand mixer to whisk until the mixture is very stiff and glossy. Finally, mix in the vanilla and it's ready.

6. Either use a palette knife or put the frosting into a piping bag and cover the whole Bundt. Use a cook's blowtorch to gently brown the marshmallow frosting. Leave to fully set for around 20 minutes and then serve. This Bundt is best eaten on the day it's made, but will keep in a cake tin for a couple of days.

Image overleaf →

# Magical Dulce De Leche Chocoflan Bundt

Magical in flavour and also in the fact that you put the chocolate batter in first and the dulce de leche custard in second and yet they switch places while cooking. What kind of wizardry is this? The answer is somewhat disappointingly prosaic, it's thanks to the chemistry between the baking powder and buttermilk.

SERVES 12

**For the 12-cup Anniversary Bundt® pan:**
20g (1 tbsp/¾oz) butter, melted

**For the cake:**
150g (1 stick + 3 tbsp) unsalted butter
200g (1 cup/7oz) light muscovado sugar
1 egg
200ml (¾ cup/7fl oz) buttermilk
1 tsp vanilla bean paste
200g (1¼ cups/7oz) plain flour
1 tsp baking powder
1 bicarbonate of soda
50g (½ cup/1¾oz) cocoa powder

**For the flan layer:**
1 x 340g (1 cup/11¾oz) can evaporated milk
1 x 397g (1 cup /14oz) can sweetened condensed milk
125g (½ cup + 1 tbsp/4½oz) cream cheese, room temperature
3 eggs
50g (¼ cup/1¾oz) dulce de leche

**To decorate (optional):**
White, dark and milk chocolate curls and shavings

1. Preheat your oven to 160°C fan/180°C/350°F/gas 4.

2. Use a pastry brush to brush a 12-cup Anniversary Bundt® pan with the melted butter. Find a roasting tray large enough to fit the Bundt® pan inside and deep enough that you can pour in water halfway up the sides.

3. Take a large mixing bowl and add the butter and sugar. Cream them together, then add the egg, buttermilk and vanilla and beat until smooth. Add the flour, baking powder, bicarbonate of soda and cocoa powder and mix until combined. Spoon into the prepared pan and smooth the top with a spatula so it's as even as you can get it.

4. To make the custard flan layer, place the evaporated milk, condensed milk, cream cheese, eggs and dulce de leche in a bullet blender and process until smooth. (If you don't have a blender, you can pass the ingredients through a fine-mesh sieve.) Place the mixture in a jug and then pour it gently over the cake batter. I like to pour it over the back of a spoon to make sure it is extra gentle.

5. Place the Bundt® pan in the roasting tray and cover snugly with 2 layers of foil. Put the tray in the oven. Pour boiling water into the roasting tray so it comes halfway up the sides and then bake the Bundt for 1 hour without opening the oven door. Once baked, leave the Bundt to cool in the pan for 1 hour and then transfer to the refrigerator to chill completely for at least a few hours but ideally overnight.

6. Carefully invert the chilled Bundt on to a serving plate. You could add milk, white and dark chocolate shavings to decorate if you like. This Bundt keeps for 2–3 days in the refrigerator.

# Pretty-In-Pink Blood Orange Bundt with Blood Orange Glaze

---

I remember eating my first blood orange when I was nine and I've been hooked ever since. My sister cut one in half to show me and I remember that sense of wonderment, the shiny blush centre of so many crimson shades, and then the taste – the tartness, the zing, the extra-ness that they bring compared to a normal orange. Also in their favour is the fact that their ruby-coloured juice makes icing the prettiest shade of pink and as they can only be enjoyed when they're in season, we have to make the most of them.

SERVES 8

**For the 10-cup Heritage Bundt® pan:**
15g (1 tbsp/½oz) butter
15g (1 tbsp/½oz) plain flour

**For the cake:**
250g (1¼ cups/9oz) caster sugar
Zest of 2 blood oranges, plus extra to serve (optional), plus 3 tbsp juice
3 eggs
125ml (½ cup/4fl oz) vegetable oil
100ml (⅓ cup + 1 tbsp/3½fl oz) soured cream
1 tsp vanilla bean paste
250g (1½ cups/9oz) self-raising flour
A pinch of salt

1. Preheat your oven to 160°C fan/180°C/350°F/gas 4.

2. Add the sugar and blood orange zest to a medium bowl. Rub the zest into the sugar to release its flavour and set aside to infuse.

3. Melt the butter, then use a pastry brush to brush it evenly over the inside of a 10-cup Heritage Bundt® pan, being careful to get into every nook and cranny. I find it easier to brush from the base up to prevent any butter pooling. Sift over the flour, moving the pan from side to side to coat it evenly. Turn it upside down and give it a final tap to remove any excess, then set aside.

4. Add the flavoured sugar, eggs, oil, soured cream, vanilla and orange juice to a large bowl and whisk to combine. Add the flour and salt and mix again until just combined. Pour the batter into the prepared pan and bake for 40–45 minutes or until a skewer inserted into the cake comes out clean.

5. To make the sugar syrup, place the sugar, vanilla and blood orange juice in a small pan over a medium heat and once the sugar has dissolved, increase the heat and simmer until the syrup has reduced by half. Set aside until ready to use.

Ingredients and method continued overleaf →

*Pretty-In-Pink Blood Orange Bundt with Blood Orange Glaze, continued*

**For the vanilla blood orange sugar syrup:**
50g (½ cup/1¾oz) caster sugar
1 tsp vanilla bean paste
100ml (⅓ cup + 1 tbsp/3½fl oz) strained blood orange juice

**For the blood orange glaze:**
45ml (3 tbsp) strained blood orange juice
125g (1 cup/4½oz) icing sugar, sifted

6. While the cake is cooling in the pan, pierce holes with a toothpick and brush the base with the sugar syrup. Once cool enough to handle, invert the cake onto a wire rack and brush the syrup all over the top.

7. When the cake has completely cooled, make the glaze by simply mixing the blood orange juice into the sifted icing sugar. Pour the glaze over the Bundt and then leave for 10 minutes to set. You can also decorate the top with extra zest, if you like. This cake will keep for a few days in an airtight container.

*Tip – If blood oranges aren't in season, you can use regular oranges. They won't turn the glaze pink but it will still taste deliciously fragrant.*

# White Chocolate & Coconut Bundt

Apparently Tom Cruise orders hundreds of coconut Bundts to be sent out to his friends and family every year at Christmas. I'm not on Tom's list, so I thought I'd create a version of my own. I haven't tasted one from the Doan's Bakery in California but if it's anything like this one, I can see why it's his Christmas cake of choice.

SERVES 12

**For the 12-cup Anniversary Bundt® pan:**
15g (1 tbsp/ ½oz) butter
15g (1 tbsp/ ½oz) plain flour

**For the cake:**
135g (¾ cup/4¾oz) creamed coconut
240g (1 cup + 1 tbsp/8¾oz) unsalted butter, softened
375g (1¾ cups + 2 tbsp/13oz) caster sugar
4 eggs
1 tsp vanilla bean paste
200ml (¾ cup/7fl oz) soured cream
100g (¾ cup/3½oz) white chocolate chips
375g (2½ cups + 2 tbsp/13oz) plain flour
2 tsp baking powder
1 tsp bicarbonate of soda
¼ tsp salt

1. Preheat your oven to 160°C fan/180°C/350°F/gas 4.

2. Melt the butter, then use a pastry brush to brush it evenly over the inside of a 12-cup Anniversary Bundt® pan, being careful to get into every nook and cranny. I find it easier to brush from the base up to prevent any butter pooling. Sift over the flour, moving the pan from side to side to coat it evenly. Turn it upside down and give it a final tap to remove any excess, then set aside.

3. Heat the creamed coconut until soft and then add to a large mixing bowl with the butter and sugar. Using hand-held electric beaters or a stand mixer, mix until smooth. Add the eggs one at a time along with the vanilla. Pour in the soured cream and then add the chocolate chips, flour, baking powder, bicarbonate of soda and salt. Pour into the prepared pan and bake for 50–55 minutes or until a skewer inserted into the cake comes out clean. Leave to cool in the pan for 15 minutes and then invert onto a wire rack to cool completely.

Ingredients and method continued overleaf →

*White Chocolate & Coconut Bundt, continued*

**For the coconut frosting:**
65g (⅓ cup/2¼oz) white chocolate
35g (2 tbsp/1¼oz) coconut cream
35g (2 tbsp/1¼oz) unsalted butter, softened
65g (⅓ cup/2¼oz) cream cheese
330g (2⅓ cups/11½oz) icing sugar
2 tbsp milk (optional)

**To decorate:**
150g (2 cups/5½oz) desiccated coconut, plus extra to coat the strawberries (optional)
250g (2 cups/9oz) fresh strawberries (optional)
75g (cups/2¾oz) white chocolate, melted (optional)

4. To make the frosting, melt the white chocolate and coconut cream together in a small pan. Add them to a bowl with the butter and cream cheese. Mix until smooth and then gradually add the icing sugar. If it seems too thick, you can add a splash of milk if needed. Once smooth, spread over the whole Bundt and then cover with desiccated coconut.

5. If you want to add more decoration, dip the strawberries in the melted white chocolate and then the coconut and fill the centre of the Bundt with them before serving. This Bundt keeps really well for up to 5 days in an airtight container.

# Movie Night Salted Caramel & Popcorn Bundt

Apart from the sculptural quality, another joy of a Bundt® pan is that hole of nothingness in the centre. It provides an opportunity to add something fun and quirky to delight and amuse. As well as being a deliciously tender caramel cake, the popcorn adds the 'salted' to the title and turns this into a Bundt to bring you back for more. Put it on the coffee table while you watch a movie and everyone can help themselves.

**SERVES 8**

**For the 10-cup Brilliance Bundt® pan:**
15g (1 tbsp/½oz) butter
15g (1 tbsp/½oz) plain flour

**For the caramel:**
250g (2 cups/9oz) caster sugar
350ml (2 cups/12fl oz) water

**For the cake:**
250g (2 sticks + 2 tbsp/9oz) unsalted butter, softened
250g (1¼ cups/9oz) caster sugar
150g (⅔ cup/5½oz) caramel
4 eggs
1 tsp vanilla bean paste
250g (2 cups/9oz) self-raising flour
250ml (1¼ cups/9floz) whole milk

1. Preheat your oven to 160°C fan/180°C/350°F/gas 4.

2. Melt the butter, then use a pastry brush to brush it evenly over the inside of a 10-cup Brilliance Bundt® pan, being careful to get into every nook and cranny. I find it easier to brush from the base up to prevent any butter pooling. Sift over the flour, moving the pan from side to side to coat it evenly. Turn it upside down and give it a final tap to remove any excess, then set aside.

3. To make the caramel, place the sugar and half the water in a saucepan over a low heat. When the sugar has dissolved, turn up the heat and, without stirring, watch the colour change to a light amber. Swirl it gently so it doesn't get too dark. Once the whole surface has turned amber, add the remaining water. (Be careful as the caramel may spit.) Whisk the caramel until smooth and calm. Pour into a clean bowl and set aside until ready to use.

**For the frosting:**
25g unsalted butter
1 tsp vanilla bean paste
150g (½ cup/5½oz) caramel
50ml milk, to loosen
300g (10½oz) icing sugar, sifted

**To decorate:**
70g (11 cups/2¾oz) salted
popcorn

4. Place the butter and sugar in the bowl of a stand mixer and mix until pale, fluffy and starting to look like a mousse. Add the caramel and mix again. Whisk the eggs and vanilla in a separate bowl and then add gradually to the batter, still mixing. When the batter is homogenous, add one-third of the flour. Mix until just combined. Add half the milk and mix until combined. Repeat with the next third of flour and the remaining milk. End with the final third of flour. Once combined, pour into the prepared pan and bake for 45–50 minutes or until the top is golden, the cake is starting to pull away from the sides and a skewer inserted into the cake comes out clean. Leave to cool in the pan on a wire rack for 15 minutes so the air can circulate all around the Bundt before inverting onto the wire rack to cool completely.

5. To make the frosting, whisk together the butter, vanilla, caramel and milk and then sift in the icing sugar. Once the consistency is thick but still soft, pour it over the top of the Bundt, or apply it with a piping bag. Decorate by filling the centre with an overflowing mound of salted popcorn. This Bundt will keep for several days in an airtight container without the popcorn.

Image overleaf →

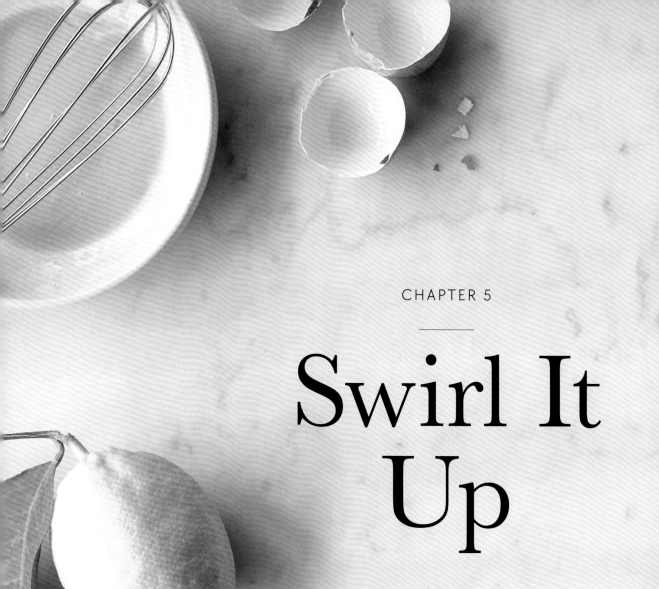

CHAPTER 5

# Swirl It Up

# Easiest Chocolate & Vanilla Marble Bundt with Milk Chocolate Glaze

This is the classic Bundt that I grew up with in Austria, except my grandmother called it a *kugelhupf*. It has the same buttery swirls of vanilla and chocolate and it was served any time of day – breakfast, afternoon tea, or in the evening – which I think is very civilised.

SERVES 8

**For the 10-cup Bundt® pan:**
15g (1 tbsp/½oz) butter
15g (1 tbsp/½oz) cocoa powder

**For the cake:**
50g (½ cup/1¾oz) cocoa powder
100ml (½ cup/3½fl oz) boiling water
250g (2 sticks + 2 tbsp/9oz) unsalted butter
300g (1½ cups/10½oz) golden caster sugar
4 eggs
1 tsp vanilla bean paste
A pinch of salt
175g (1¼ cups/6oz) plain flour
2 tsp baking powder

**For the milk chocolate glaze:**
175g (1 cup/6oz) milk chocolate
110g (1 stick/3¾oz) unsalted butter
1 tbsp golden syrup

**To decorate:**
Milk chocolate curls

1. Preheat your oven to 160°C fan/180°C/350°F/gas 4.

2. Melt the butter, then use a pastry brush to brush it evenly over the inside of a 10-cup Bundt® pan, being careful to get into every nook and cranny. I find it easier to brush from the base up to prevent any butter pooling. Sift over the cocoa powder, moving the pan from side to side to coat it evenly. Turn it upside down and give it a final tap to remove any excess, then set aside.

3. To a small bowl, add the cocoa powder and boiling water and mix until you have a smooth paste. Set aside to cool.

4. Add the butter and sugar to a mixing bowl and cream together until pale and fluffy. Add the eggs one at time, beating well between each addition, followed by the vanilla and salt. Fold through the flour and baking powder and then mix until just combined. Pour half the mixture into a separate bowl and add the cocoa paste to it. Mix until smooth.

5. Pour a layer of one of the batters into the prepared pan and then add a layer of the other colour, repeating until you've used all the batter. Drag a skewer through the mixture and swirl it gently around. Bake for 50 minutes or until a skewer inserted into the cake comes out clean. Leave the Bundt to cool in the pan for 10 minutes before inverting onto a wire rack to cool completely.

6. Melt the chocolate, butter and golden syrup together in a small saucepan (or in a heatproof bowl in the microwave) and then pour over the Bundt. Allow to set, then decorate with chocolate curls and serve. This Bundt will keep for up to 5 days in an airtight container.

# Easy Chocolate Hazelnut Bundt

Why are the most fabulous things to eat the same things we mustn't indulge too heavily in? There is, however, always room for a treat in moderation and this is mine. A super-tender simple Bundt that can be enjoyed with a cup of tea.

SERVES 12

**For the 12-cup Bundt® pan:**
15g (1 tbsp/ ½oz) butter
15g (1 tbsp/ ½oz) cocoa powder

**For the cake:**
325g (3 sticks/11 ½oz) unsalted butter, softened
500g (2 ¼ cups/1lb 2oz) caster sugar
5 eggs
1 tsp vanilla bean paste
100ml (½ cup/3 ½fl oz) buttermilk
360g (3 cups/12 ½oz) plain flour
2 tsp baking powder
150g (½ cup/5 ½oz) chocolate hazelnut spread (I use Nutella)

**For the chocolate hazelnut buttercream:**
125g (½ cup/4 ½oz) cream cheese
150g (½ cup/5 ½oz) chocolate hazelnut spread
60g (¼ cup/1 ¾oz) unsalted butter
A pinch of salt
400g (2 ¾ cups/14oz) icing sugar

**To decorate:**
50g (⅓ cup/1 ¾oz) hazelnuts, chopped

1. Preheat your oven to 160°C fan/180°C/350°F/gas 4.

2. Melt the butter, then use a pastry brush to brush it evenly over the inside of a 12-cup Bundt® pan, being careful to get into every nook and cranny. I find it easier to brush from the base up to prevent any butter pooling. Sift over the cocoa powder, moving the pan from side to side to coat it evenly. Turn it upside down and give it a final tap to remove any excess, then set aside.

3. Cream the butter and sugar together in a large mixing bowl. Add the eggs, vanilla and buttermilk, mix again and then fold through the flour and baking powder. Mix until just combined.

4. Divide the batter between 2 bowls and add the chocolate hazelnut spread to one of them. Mix it through until evenly coloured. Add spoonfuls of the batter to the prepared pan, alternating between chocolate hazelnut and vanilla. Take a skewer or toothpick and drag it though the batter to create swirls. Bake for 50–55 minutes or until a skewer inserted into the cake comes out clean. Leave to cool in the pan for 15 minutes and then invert onto a wire rack to cool completely.

5. To make the frosting, place the cream cheese, chocolate hazelnut spread, butter, salt and icing sugar in a mixing bowl and use hand-held electric beaters to mix it until smooth and velvety. Use a palette knife to spread the frosting over the top of the Bundt and then scatter over the chopped hazelnuts. This Bundt will keep for several days in an airtight container.

# Lemon & Raspberry Yoghurt Bundt with Raspberry Mascarpone Glaze

---

Best friends lemon and raspberry are just hanging out together in this tenderest of cakes.

SERVES 8

**For the 10-cup Swirl Bundt® pan:**
15g (1 tbsp/ ½oz) butter
15g (1 tbsp/ ½oz) plain flour

**For the cake:**
325g (3 sticks/12oz) unsalted butter, softened
500g (2¼ cups/1lb 2oz) caster sugar
6 eggs
1 tsp vanilla bean paste
100g (⅓ cup/3½oz) Greek yoghurt
360g (3 cups/12½oz) plain flour
2 tsp baking powder
Zest of 1 lemon, plus 1 tbsp juice
50g (⅓ cup/1¾oz) freeze-dried raspberry powder (or crushed freeze-fried raspberries)
½ tsp pink food colouring

**For the mascarpone frosting:**
150g (⅔ cup/5½oz) mascarpone
170g (¾ cup/6oz) icing sugar
A squeeze of lemon
50g (½ cup/1¾oz) fresh raspberries

**To decorate:**
Fresh raspberries

1. Preheat your oven to 160°C fan/180°C/350°F/gas 4.

2. Melt the butter, then use a pastry brush to brush it evenly over the inside of a 10-cup Swirl Bundt® pan, being careful to get into every nook and cranny. I find it easier to brush from the base up to prevent any butter pooling. Sift over the flour, moving the pan from side to side to coat it evenly. Turn it upside down and give it a final tap to remove any excess, then set aside.

3. In a large mixing bowl, combine the softened butter and sugar. Add the eggs and vanilla bean paste and continue to beat until fully incorporated. Add the yoghurt and mix it in, followed by the flour and baking powder. Beat until just combined.

4. Divide the mixture in two and add the lemon zest and juice to one bowl and the raspberry powder and pink food colouring to the other. Add heaped spoonfuls of each mixture alternately to the prepared pan and then drag a skewer through to create a marbled effect. Bake for 50–55 minutes. Leave to cool in the pan for 10 minutes and then invert onto a wire rack to cool completely.

5. Mix the mascarpone, icing sugar and lemon juice together and then fold through the raspberries, gently squashing them so they add a ripple. Place the Bundt on a serving plate and spoon over the mascarpone frosting. Arrange raspberries around the top and serve. Once iced, it's best to store this Bundt in a refrigerator and bring to room temperature when serving.

# Matcha & Vanilla Bundt
# with White Chocolate

My sister Sam came home from Japan singing the praises of Japanese bakeries and how incredible all things matcha were there and given she left London not being particularly partial to the stuff, I was intrigued. She was my chief taste tester for this recipe because I had to get it just right. First I ordered the wrong kind, then I used the wrong amount, but once I got some ceremonial grade matcha I was on the right track and with a few more tweaks I arrived at this delicious recipe.

SERVES 8

**For the 10-cup Bundt® pan:**
15g (1 tbsp/ ½oz) butter
15g (1 tbsp/ ½oz) plain flour

**For the cake:**
225g (1 cup/8oz) unsalted
    butter, softened
225g (1 cup/8oz) caster sugar
5 eggs, lightly beaten
1 tsp vanilla extract
A pinch of salt
275g (2 cups/9¾oz) self-
    raising flour
100ml (½ cup/3½fl oz) whole
    milk, warmed
3 tbsp (20g/¾oz) matcha
    powder (ceremonial grade)

**To decorate:**
85g (½ cup/3oz) white chocolate
85g (½ cup/3oz) milk chocolate
6 tbsp double cream

*Tip – Style with pretty pink blossom flowers, if you like. The matcha must be ceremonial grade rather than culinary otherwise you won't get the same bright green colour.*

1. Preheat your oven to 160°C fan/180°C/350°F/gas 4.

2. Melt the butter, then use a pastry brush to brush it evenly over the inside of a 10-cup Bundt® pan, being careful to get into every nook and cranny. I find it easier to brush from the base up to prevent any butter pooling. Sift over the flour, moving the pan from side to side to coat it evenly. Turn it upside down and give it a final tap to remove any excess, then set aside.

3. Place the butter and sugar in a large bowl and mix with hand-held electric beaters until pale and fluffy. Add the eggs, a little at a time, mixing to combine. Add the vanilla and mix to combine. Add one-third of the flour and the salt and mix briefly, then add half the milk and mix. Repeat again and end with the final third of flour. Mix until just combined and smooth. Place one-third of the mixture in a separate bowl and add the matcha powder to it. Mix until the colour is uniform. Add half of the vanilla mixture to the prepared pan, followed by alternate large dollops of the matcha and vanilla mixtures. Bake for 45 minutes or until a skewer inserted into the cake comes out clean and the cake comes away from the sides of the pan. Leave to cool in the pan for 10 minutes and then invert onto a wire rack to cool completely.

4. To make the glaze, break the white chocolate into pieces and place in a heatproof bowl, do the same with the milk chocolate in a separate bowl. Heat the cream either in a small saucepan or in a bowl in the microwave. Pour half the hot cream over the chocolate in each of the bowls. Wait a few minutes for the chocolate to melt and then stir with a fork or small whisk until smooth. Use a fork to create lines all around the Bundt with both the melted white and milk chocolate until the entire Bundt is covered.

# Spiced Chai & Maple Cheesecake Bundt with Spiced Chai Glaze

Perfectly tender, there's so much to love in this bake of autumn flavours. The spiced chai Bundt is generously swirled with maple-scented cream cheese and topped with a sweet glaze.

SERVES 8

**For the 10-cup Bundt® pan:**
15g (1 tbsp/ ½oz) butter
15g (1 tbsp/ ½oz) plain flour

**For the spiced chai blend:**
1 tsp ground cardamon
1 tsp ground cinnamon
1 tsp ground ginger
½ tsp ground cloves
½ tsp ground nutmeg
A small pinch of ground pepper

**For the cake:**
235g (1 cup + 2 tbsp/8½oz) soft light brown sugar
210g (1½ cups/7½oz) plain flour
2 tsp baking powder
1 tsp bicarbonate of soda
150ml (¾ cup/5fl oz) whole milk
175g (¾ cup/6oz) unsalted butter, melted
3 eggs

**For the maple cheesecake swirl:**
1 egg yolk
240g (1¼ cups/8½oz) cream cheese
5 tbsp maple syrup

**For the spiced chai glaze:**
175g (1¼ cups/6oz) icing sugar
4 tbsp whole milk

1. Preheat your oven to 160°C fan/180°C/350°F/gas 4.

2. Melt the butter, then use a pastry brush to brush it evenly over the inside of a 10-cup Bundt® pan, being careful to get into every nook and cranny. I find it easier to brush from the base up to prevent any butter pooling. Sift over the flour, moving the pan from side to side to coat it evenly. Turn it upside down and give it a final tap to remove any excess, then set aside.

3. Mix the maple cheesecake swirl ingredients together in a medium-sized bowl and then chill until ready to use.

4. Mix the spices together in a small bowl. You can be slightly flexible with the blend and work with what you have to hand; if there's a spice you don't like, it won't affect the end result if you leave it out. Add half the spices to a mixing bowl along with the sugar, flour, baking powder and bicarbonate of soda. Whisk to combine.

5. In a separate bowl, whisk the milk, melted butter and eggs together and then pour over the dry ingredients. Whisk until smooth. Pour the spiced chai batter into the prepared pan and then simply pour the cream cheese and maple syrup mixture on to the batter – it will swirl itself during baking. Bake for 45 minutes or until a skewer inserted into the cake comes out clean. Leave to cool in the pan for 30 minutes, so the cream cheese can really set.

6. To make the glaze, put the remaining spices into a bowl with the icing sugar. Use a small whisk to combine. Add the milk and whisk until you have a smooth, pourable glaze. Once the Bundt cake has cooled, pour the glaze all over the top. Serve with a cup of chai tea! This Bundt will keep for a couple of days in an airtight container.

# Red Velvet Cheesecake Bundt with Cream Cheese Swirl

Red velvet is always a winner and rather than having a layer of cream cheese frosting through the centre this one has a swirl built in. It's such a celebration of chocolate and yet it isn't overly chocolatey, and with the tang from the buttermilk it all sings together.

SERVES 8

**For the 10-cup Swirl Bundt® pan:**
15g (1 tbsp/ ½oz) butter
15g (1 tbsp/ ½oz) plain flour

**For the cream cheese swirl:**
360g (1¾ cups/ 12½oz) cream cheese
75g (5 tbsp/ 2¾oz) caster sugar
1 large egg
1 tsp vanilla bean paste

**For the cake:**
350g (1 ½ cups/ 12oz) unsalted butter, softened
450g (2½ cups/ 1lb) caster sugar
1 tbsp vanilla bean paste
6 eggs
350g (2 ⅔ cups/ 12oz) self-raising flour
A pinch of salt
100g (1 cup/ 3 ½oz) cocoa powder
250ml (1 ¼ cups/ 9fl oz) buttermilk
1 tbsp red food colouring paste (or more depending on the brand you're using)

1. Preheat your oven to 160°C fan/180°C/350°F/gas 4.

2. Melt the butter, then use a pastry brush to brush it evenly over the inside of a 10-cup Swirl Bundt® pan, being careful to get into every nook and cranny. I find it easier to brush from the base up to prevent any butter pooling. Sift over the flour, moving the pan from side to side to coat it evenly. Turn it upside down and give it a final tap to remove any excess, then set aside.

3. To make the swirl, mix the cream cheese, sugar, egg and vanilla together in a bowl and chill until ready to use.

4. To make the red velvet cake, put the butter and sugar into the bowl of a stand mixer. Cream them together until pale and fluffy and then add the vanilla and the eggs, one at a time. Add the flour, salt and cocoa powder alternately with the buttermilk, ending with flour, mixing between each addition until you have a smooth batter. Pour the batter into the prepared pan and then add ice-cream scoops of the cream cheese mixture on top (they'll sink while baking). Drag a toothpick through the mixture to create the swirls. Bake for 50–55 minutes or until a skewer inserted into the cake comes out clean. Leave to cool in the pan for 15 minutes and then invert onto a wire rack to cool completely.

**For the cream cheese frosting (optional):**

50g (¼ cup/1¾oz) cream cheese

25g (2 tbsp/1oz) unsalted butter, softened

200g (1½ cups/7oz) icing sugar

1 tbsp whole milk (optional, to loosen slightly)

**For the icing:**

45ml (3 tbsp) water

125g (1 cup/4½oz) icing sugar, sifted

5. To make the frosting, mix the cream cheese, butter and icing sugar together until smooth, adding the milk if needed to make it spreadable. Use a palette knife or piping bag to cover the top of the cooled Bundt with the frosting. Alternatively to decorate with a simple glaze, mix the water and sifted icing sugar together with a small whisk and then pour or drizzle over the cooled Bundt and leave for 10 minutes to set. Due to the cream cheese swirl, this Bundt is best eaten on the day it's made and stored in the refrigerator.

Glazed image overleaf →

# Peanut Butter & Jelly Bundt

———

A favourite flavour combination in our house but I wanted to see if I could bring some elegance to a classic PB&J. So I came up with this peanut butter frosting and it's so light and fluffy with such a subtle flavour that you can't help but love it.

SERVES 12

**For the 10-cup Bundt® pan:**
15g (1 tbsp/ ½oz) butter
15g (1 tbsp/ ½oz) plain flour

**For the cake:**
250g (2 sticks + 2 tbsp/9oz)
  unsalted butter, softened
75g (⅓ cup/2¾oz) smooth
  peanut butter
325g (1⅔ cups/11½oz)
  golden caster sugar
4 eggs
1 tsp vanilla bean paste
200ml (1 cup/7fl oz) soured
  cream
250g (1½ cups/9oz) self-
  raising flour

**For the filling:**
4 tbsp strawberry jam
4 tbsp smooth peanut butter

1. Preheat your oven to 160°C fan/180°C/350°F/gas 4.

2. Melt the butter, then use a pastry brush to brush it evenly over the inside of a 10-cup Bundt® pan, being careful to get into every nook and cranny. I find it easier to brush from the base up to prevent any butter pooling. Sift over the flour, moving the pan from side to side to coat it evenly. Turn it upside down and give it a final tap to remove any excess, then set aside.

3. Place the softened butter in a mixing bowl and cream with the peanut butter and caster sugar. Add the eggs, vanilla and soured cream and mix again until homogenous. Fold through the flour and then pour into the prepared pan. Bake for 45–50 minutes or until a skewer inserted into the cake comes out clean. Leave to cool in the pan for 15 minutes and then invert onto a wire rack to cool completely.

4. When the Bundt has cooled, slice it half horizontally and lift off the top half. Spread one cut side with strawberry jam and the other with peanut butter, then sandwich them back together.

**For the peanut butter frosting:**
4 egg whites
400g (2 cups/14oz) caster sugar
500g (2¼ cups/1lb 5oz)
   unsalted butter, room
   temperature
90g (½ cup/3¼oz) smooth
   peanut butter

**To decorate:**
100g (⅔ cup/3½oz) salted,
   unroasted peanuts
8 fresh strawberries, plus extra
   for the centre

5. To make the frosting, add the egg whites and sugar to the bowl of a stand mixer. Mix them together and then place the bowl over a saucepan of simmering water over a medium heat. Heat the egg whites and sugar until you can no longer feel sugar grains between your fingertips (taking care not to burn yourself), or the mixture reaches 80°C (176°F) on a sugar thermometer. It will take around 5 minutes. Put the bowl under your stand mixer and whisk the egg whites until very stiff, for about another 5 minutes. With the mixer on a medium speed, add the butter a tablespoon at a time until it's fully incorporated. If you find the mixture thins, just keep going, because when it cools down it will thicken again. If it seems very thin, simply put it in the refrigerator to cool and then beat again. Once the butter is all incorporated, whisk through the peanut butter. The flavour is subtle, so you can add more if you want it stronger.

6. Use a palette knife to spread the frosting generously over the entire Bundt, or you can fill a piping bag and really get creative. Scatter over the peanuts and arrange fresh strawberries in the centre and around the Bundt. This Bundt needs to be refrigerated but could be made the day before and then brought to room temperature before serving.

# Chocolate, Rose & Pistachio Bundt with Chocolate Ganache

Possibly the prettiest Bundt of all, which means you have to share it. You couldn't possibly hide all that Bundt beauty under a bushel. Make it for the school fair or take it to that coffee morning and everyone will think you've done something clever when in fact it couldn't be easier.

SERVES 12

**For the 12-cup Anniversary Braided Bundt® pan:**
15g (1 tbsp/ ½oz) butter
15g (1 tbsp/ ½oz) cocoa powder

**For the cake:**
325g (3 sticks/11oz) unsalted butter, melted
500g (2¼ cups/1lb 2oz) caster sugar
5 eggs
1 tsp vanilla bean paste
360g (3 cups/12½oz) plain flour
2 tsp baking powder
100ml (½ cup/3½fl oz) whole milk
50g (⅓ cup/1¾oz) cocoa powder
75ml (⅓ cup/2½fl oz) boiling water
50g (¼ cup/1¾oz) pistachio paste (see page 18)
1 tsp rose water
Pink and green food colouring

1. Preheat your oven to 160°C fan/180°C/350°F/gas 4.

2. Melt the butter, then use a pastry brush to brush it evenly over the inside of a 12-cup Anniversary Braided Bundt® pan, being careful to get into every nook and cranny. I find it easier to brush from the base up to prevent any butter pooling. Sift over the cocoa powder, moving the pan from side to side to coat it evenly. Turn it upside down and give it a final tap to remove any excess, then set aside.

3. Combine the butter and sugar in a large bowl using hand-held electric beaters. Add the eggs and vanilla and continue to beat until fully incorporated. Add one-third of the flour and the baking powder followed by half the milk, repeat, and then add the final third of flour. Beat until just combined. Divide the mixture evenly between 3 bowls.

4. In a small bowl, whisk together the cocoa powder and boiling water until you have a paste and add it to one bowl of the mixture, mixing well so the colour is even. Add the rose water and pink food colouring to the next bowl, and the pistachio paste and green food colouring to the last bowl. Mix each one well so the colour is uniform. Spoon the different mixtures into the prepared pan, roughly layering the colours on top of one another. Keep repeating until you have used up all the mixture. Drag a toothpick gently through to swirl the mixture. Bake for 50–55 minutes or until a skewer inserted into the cake comes out clean. Leave to cool in the pan for 10 minutes and then invert onto a wire rack to cool completely.

**For the chocolate ganache:**
100g (½ cup/3½oz) dark
  chocolate
1 tbsp melted butter
1 tbsp golden syrup
150ml (⅔ cup/5fl oz) double
  cream

**To decorate:**
Edible rose petals
Chopped pistachios
Chocolate shavings

5. Once the Bundt has cooled, prepare the ganache. Put the chocolate in a bowl with the butter and golden syrup. Heat the double cream to near boiling and then pour over the bowl of chocolate. Leave for a few minutes to melt and then use a fork to mix until smooth.

6. Place a plate under the cooling rack and then pour the dark chocolate ganache over the Bundt. Decorate with edible rose petals, chopped pistachios and chocolate shavings and serve. This will keep for a couple of days in an airtight container.

---

*Variation: To make a Neapolitan Bundt, simply leave out the pistachio paste and replace the rose water with a few tablespoons of freeze-dried raspberry powder.*

Image overleaf →

# Salted Miso Caramel Bundt with Miso Caramel Cream Cheese Frosting

Miso caramel really is all that you have probably heard it is. It's your usual sweet and fabulous caramel but with an umami background note that creeps in, taking it to the next level. I keep a jar in my refrigerator (and have to resist eating it by the spoonful!).

SERVES 8

**For the 10-cup Bundt® pan:**
15g (1 tbsp/½oz) butter
15g (1 tbsp/½oz) plain flour

**For the cake:**
300g (2½ sticks/1⅓ cups/ 10½oz) unsalted butter
200g (1 cup/7oz) caster sugar
4 eggs
1 tsp vanilla bean paste
200g (1¼ cups/7oz) self-raising flour
½ tsp baking powder
½ tsp bicarbonate of soda
A pinch of salt

**For the miso caramel and cream cheese frosting:**
200ml (¾ cup + 2 tbsp/7fl oz) double cream
300g (1½ cups/10½oz) soft light brown sugar
100g (6¼ tbsp/3½oz) white miso paste
150g (¾ cup/5½oz) cream cheese

1. Preheat your oven to 160°C fan/180°C/350°F/gas 4.

2. Melt the butter, then use a pastry brush to brush it evenly over the inside of a 10-cup Bundt® pan, being careful to get into every nook and cranny. I find it easier to brush from the base up to prevent any butter pooling. Sift over the flour, moving the pan from side to side to coat it evenly. Turn it upside down and give it a final tap to remove any excess, then set aside.

3. To make the miso caramel, add the double cream, sugar and miso paste to a small saucepan. Gently whisk everything together over a gentle heat until smooth and then turn up the heat to bring it to a gentle simmer for 2 minutes to thicken. Pour into a bowl to cool and set aside until ready to use.

4. Place the butter and sugar in a medium bowl and cream together until pale and fluffy. Break the eggs into a small bowl and whisk them together with the vanilla. Pour them gradually into the creamed butter and sugar and mix until fully combined. Sift over the flour, baking powder, bicarbonate of soda and salt and fold until just combined. Spoon a quarter of the batter into a separate bowl and then pour over 150g (⅔ cup/5½oz) of the miso caramel. Mix it through until even in colour. Pour half of the vanilla batter into the prepared pan and the pour over the miso caramel batter, followed by the remaining vanilla batter. Use a skewer to swirl them together. Bake for 45–50 minutes or until a skewer inserted into the cake comes out clean. Leave to cool in the pan for 10–15 minutes, then invert onto a wire rack to cool completely.

5. Once the Bundt has cooled, make the icing by adding most of the remaining miso caramel and cream cheese to a bowl and whisk them together. Spoon over the top of the Bundt and then add an indulgent extra drizzle of miso caramel just before serving. This Bundt will keep for a few days in an airtight container but refrigerate if in a warm environment.

# Strawberries & Cream Bundt

Strawberries and cream is a classic flavour combination, so whenever I go to a pick-your-own farm I always get really over enthusiastic and pick far too many. This is a great bake to celebrate the strawberry season and really enjoy them while they're at their peak.

SERVES 8

**For the 10-cup Bundt® pan:**
15g (1 tbsp/ ½oz) butter
15g (1 tbsp/ ½oz) plain flour

**For the cake:**
200g (2 cups/7oz) fresh
   strawberries (or use freeze-
   dried powder)
225g (1 cup/8oz) unsalted
   butter, softened
275g (1 ½ cups/9¾oz) golden
   caster sugar
4 eggs
1 tsp vanilla bean paste
225g (1 ½ cups/8oz) self-
   raising flour
75ml (⅓ cup/2 ½fl oz) single
   cream
½ tsp pink food colouring

**For the strawberry frosting:**
4 tbsp freeze-dried
   strawberries
100g (½ cup/3 ½oz) cream
   cheese
50g (3 ½ tbsp/1 ¾oz) unsalted
   butter
300g (2 cups/10 ½oz) icing
   sugar

**To decorate:**
Freeze-dried strawberries
Fresh strawberries

1. Preheat your oven to 160°C fan/180°C/350°F/gas 4.

2. Melt the butter, then use a pastry brush to brush it evenly over the inside of a 10-cup Bundt® pan, being careful to get into every nook and cranny. I find it easier to brush from the base up to prevent any butter pooling. Sift over the flour, moving the pan from side to side to coat it evenly. Turn it upside down and give it a final tap to remove any excess, then set aside.

3. Place the strawberries in a small saucepan and cook them gently for about 25 minutes until they break up into a purée and become syrupy and thickened. Set aside to cool and then chill until ready to use. This can be done the day before baking and needs to be stored in the refrigerator.

4. Place the butter and sugar in a large bowl and use hand-held electric beaters to mix together until pale and fluffy. Add the eggs, one at a time, mixing after each addition, then add the vanilla. Add half the flour, mix until just combined and then pour in the cream. Add the remaining flour and mix until just combined and smooth. Divide the mixture in half and add the strawberry compote to one half. Mix it in and add the pink food colouring to deepen the pink tone. Pour half the vanilla mixture into the prepared pan, then half the pink mixture, half the vanilla and half the pink. Use a toothpick to swirl it around. Bake for 40 minutes or until a skewer inserted into the cake comes out clean. Leave to cool in the pan for 10 minutes and then invert onto a wire rack to cool completely.

5. To make the frosting, bash the freeze-dried strawberries to a powder and then add to a bowl with the cream cheese, butter and icing sugar. Beat until smooth and then pipe the frosting over the Bundt or use a palette knife to spread it over. Decorate with strawberries to serve. This Bundt is best eaten the day it's made but will keep until the following day.

# Browned Butter, Cream Cheese & Cinnamon Pecan Bundt

A sweet, warming slice of this is the perfect autumn treat. Beyond delicious and so simple to make, with pecan crunch running through in the swirl.

SERVES 8

**For the 10-cup Bundt® pan:**
15g (1 tbsp/ ½oz) butter
15g (1 tbsp/ ½oz) plain flour

**For the pecan swirl:**
125g (1 cup/4 ½oz) pecans, chopped
150g (¾ cup/5 ½oz) soft light brown sugar
1 tsp ground cinnamon
180g (1 cup/6oz) cream cheese

**For the cake:**
250g (2 sticks + 2 tbsp/9oz) unsalted butter
325g (2 cups/11 ½oz) golden caster sugar
4 eggs
1 tsp vanilla bean paste
75ml (⅓ cup/2½fl oz) buttermilk
A pinch of salt
275g (2 cups/9¾oz) self-raising flour

**For the browned butter frosting:**
75g (⅓ cup/2¾oz) unsalted butter
320g (2 cups + 2 tbsp/11 ½oz) icing sugar
1 tbsp whole milk (optional)

**To finish:**
A handful of pecans, roughly chopped
2 tbsp demerara sugar

1. Preheat your oven to 160°C fan/180°C/350°F/gas 4.

2. Melt the butter, then use a pastry brush to brush it evenly over the inside of a 10-cup Bundt® pan, being careful to get into every nook and cranny. I find it easier to brush from the base up to prevent any butter pooling. Sift over the flour, moving the pan from side to side to coat it evenly. Turn it upside down and give it a final tap to remove any excess, then set aside.

3. Add the pecans, sugar and cinnamon to a bowl and mix them together to let the flavours infuse. Set aside.

4. Put the butter in a non-stick frying pan and gently melt it over a low heat. Continue to heat it until it turns a gentle brown. Pour into a mixing bowl.

5. To make the Bundt, add the sugar and eggs to the browned butter and beat until smooth. Add the vanilla, buttermilk and salt and mix again. Fold though the flour until just combined and then pour half the batter into the prepared pan. Scatter over the pecan, sugar and cinnamon in a single layer and then dollop over spoonfuls of the cream cheese. Pour over the remaining batter. Bake for 50–55 minutes or until a skewer inserted into the cake comes out clean. Leave to cool in the pan for 15 minutes and then invert onto a wire rack to cool completely.

6. To make the frosting, gently melt the butter in a non-stick frying pan over a low heat and continue to heat it until it turns a gentle brown. Pour over the icing sugar and mix until smooth. Add a little milk if it seems too thick. Pour over the Bundt and then decorate with the pecans, sprinkling over the demerara sugar. This Bundt will keep for up to 5 days in an airtight container.

# Tiramisu Bundt with Chocolate Ganache & Mascarpone Frosting

All the yumminess of tiramisu but slightly reversed so there's less cream and more sponge. It works delightfully and tastes perfect with a coffee.

SERVES 8

**For the 10-cup Bundt® pan:**
15g (1 tbsp/ ½oz) butter
15g (1 tbsp/ ½oz) plain flour

**For the cake:**
225g (1 cup/8oz) unsalted butter
275g (1 ½ cups/9¾oz) golden caster sugar
1 tsp vanilla bean paste
4 eggs
225g (1¾ cups/8oz) self-raising flour
100ml (½ cup/3½fl oz) whole milk
10g (2 tbsp/ ¼oz) instant coffee
100ml (½ cup/3½fl oz) boiling water

1. Preheat your oven to 160°C fan/180°C/350°F/gas 4.

2. Melt the butter, then use a pastry brush to brush it evenly over the inside of a 10-cup Bundt® pan, being careful to get into every nook and cranny. I find it easier to brush from the base up to prevent any butter pooling. Sift over the flour, moving the pan from side to side to coat it evenly. Turn it upside down and give it a final tap to remove any excess, then set aside.

3. Place the butter into a mixing bowl and add the sugar. Cream them together until pale and fluffy. Add the vanilla and eggs and beat again. Fold in the flour and then divide the mixture in half. Add the milk to one half, then dissolve the coffee in the boiling water and add it to the other half. Add alternate spoonfuls of vanilla and coffee batter to the prepared pan. Bake for 40–45 minutes or until a skewer inserted into the cake comes out clean. Leave to cool in the pan on a wire rack for 15 minutes so the air can circulate all around it and then invert onto the wire rack to cool completely.

**For the ganache:**

75g (5 tbsp/2¾oz) dark
   chocolate, 70% cocoa solids,
   broken into pieces (or use
   chips)
50ml (¼ cup/2fl oz) double
   cream, hot

**For the mascarpone frosting:**

250ml (1 cup + 2 tbsp/9fl oz)
   double cream
250g (1¼ cups/9oz)
   mascarpone
100ml (1 cup/3½fl oz)
   Marsala
1 tsp vanilla bean paste
50g (⅓ cup/1¾oz) icing sugar

**To decorate:**

Cocoa powder
Dark chocolate

4. Place the chocolate in a small bowl and then pour over the hot cream. Leave for a few minutes to melt and then mix with a fork until smooth. Pour over the top of the Bundt and leave to set.

5. Use hand-held electric beaters to whisk the double cream and mascarpone together until thick. Pour in the Marsala, then add the vanilla bean paste and icing sugar and mix until smooth. Transfer the frosting into a piping bag and pipe all around the top of the Bundt or use a palette knife to spread it over. Dust with cocoa powder and grate chocolate over the top to decorate. This Bundt will keep for a few days in the refrigerator.

# Chocolate & Orange Bundt

———

To create a Bundt interpretation of a classic chocolate orange
biscuit meant I needed an orange jelly layer on a squishy sponge
all wrapped up in bittersweet chocolate, and this rich and
decadent Bundt hits that spot.

**SERVES 10**

**For the 10-cup Swirl
    Bundt® pan:**

15g (1 tbsp/ ½oz) butter
15g (1 tbsp/ ½oz) plain flour

**For the cake:**

325g (3 sticks/11 ½oz)
    unsalted butter, softened
500g (2 ¼ cups/1lb 2oz)
    caster sugar
5 eggs
1 tsp vanilla bean paste
100ml (½ cup/3 ½fl oz)
    buttermilk
360g (3 cups/12 ½oz)
    plain flour
2 tsp baking powder
45g (¼ cup/1 ½oz) cocoa
    powder
50ml (¼ cup/2fl oz)
    boiling water
Zest of 1 orange, plus
    3 tbsp juice

1. Preheat your oven to 160°C fan/180°C/350°F/gas 4.

2. Melt the butter, then use a pastry brush to brush it evenly over
   the inside of a 10-cup Swirl Bundt® pan, being careful to get into
   every nook and cranny. I find it easier to brush from the base up
   to prevent any butter pooling. Sift over the flour, moving the pan
   from side to side to coat it evenly. Turn it upside down and give
   it a final tap to remove any excess, then set aside.

3. Cream the butter and sugar together in a large mixing bowl.
   Add the eggs, vanilla and buttermilk, mix again and then fold
   through the flour and baking powder. Mix until just combined.
   Divide the batter between 2 bowls. Mix the cocoa powder and
   boiling water together to make a paste and add it to one bowl,
   then add the orange zest and juice to the other. Add spoonfuls
   of each mixture to the prepared pan, alternating between the
   two. Take a skewer or toothpick and drag it though the batter to
   create swirls. Bake for 50–55 minutes or until a skewer inserted
   into the cake comes out clean. Leave to cool for 15 minutes in
   the pan and then invert onto a wire rack to cool completely.

4. To make the orange jelly, melt the orange jelly in the boiling
   water, or if using orange juice, bloom the gelatine in a bowl of
   cold water and then warm the orange juice and sugar in a small
   saucepan and whisk in the gelatine. Set the jelly in a thin layer on
   a plate that is the same size as the top of the Bundt. Once set,
   cut a circle from the centre and place it on top of the cold Bundt
   – the ganache will hold it in place.

Ingredients and method continued overleaf →

**For the orange jelly:**
135g (4¾oz) orange jelly
300ml (1½ cups/10fl oz)
   boiling water

*Or*

4 platinum-grade gelatine
   leaves
300ml (1½ cups/10fl oz)
   orange juice
75g (5 tbsp/2¾oz) caster sugar

**For the chocolate ganache:**
100g (½ cup/3½oz) dark
   or bittersweet chocolate,
   70% cocoa solids
1 tbsp golden syrup
150ml (⅔ cup/5fl oz)
   double cream

**To decorate:**
Orange zest

5. To make the ganache, place the chocolate and golden syrup in a bowl. Heat the cream to almost boiling and then pour it over the chocolate and syrup. Let it sit for a few minutes to melt and then whisk until smooth. Pour the ganache over the top of the Bundt, concealing the orange jelly. Leave to set.

6. Decorate the top with orange zest. This Bundt will keep for a couple of days in an airtight container.

# Chocolate & Pumpkin Bundt with Maple Syrup Glaze

I love this autumn Bundt with its taste of pumpkin and chocolate and the pretty swirls they create, the perfect expression of the season.

SERVES 12

**For the 12-cup Anniversary Bundt® pan:**
15g (1 tbsp/ ½oz) butter
15g (1 tbsp/ ½oz) plain flour

**For the cake:**
325g (3 sticks/11½oz) unsalted butter, melted
500g (2½ cups/1lb 2oz) golden caster sugar
5 eggs
120ml (½ cup/4fl oz) soured cream
1 tsp vanilla bean paste
325g (2¾ cups/11½oz) plain flour
2 tsp baking powder
30g (3 tbsp/1oz) cocoa powder
75ml (⅓ cup/2½fl oz) boiling water
200g (¾ cup/7oz) pumpkin, cooked and puréed or canned
½ tsp each ground cinnamon, nutmeg and ginger

**For the glaze:**
225g (2 cups/8oz) icing sugar, sifted
50g (4 tbsp/1¾oz) unsalted butter
½ tsp vanilla bean paste
180ml (12 tbsp/6fl oz) maple syrup

**To decorate:**
Pumpkin seeds

1. Preheat your oven to 160°C fan/180°C/350°F/gas 4.

2. Melt the butter, then use a pastry brush to brush it evenly over the inside of a 12-cup Anniversary Bundt® pan, being careful to get into every nook and cranny. I find it easier to brush from the base up to prevent any butter pooling. Sift over the flour, moving the pan from side to side to coat it evenly. Turn it upside down and give it a final tap to remove any excess, then set aside.

3. In the bowl of a stand mixer, beat the butter and sugar together. Add the eggs, soured cream and vanilla and mix until completely combined. Fold through the flour and baking powder.

4. Place the cocoa powder in a small bowl and pour over the boiling water. Mix to a paste. Place the pumpkin purée in a separate bowl and add the spices. Mix well.

5. Divide the cake mixture in half and add the cocoa mixture to one half and the pumpkin to the other. Mix them both until homogenous. Pour half the chocolate batter into the prepared pan and then add the pumpkin batter followed by the remaining chocolate batter. Use a skewer or toothpick to swirl the batters gently together. Bake for 1 hour 10 minutes–1 hour 15 minutes or until a skewer inserted into the cake comes out clean. Leave to cool in the pan on a wire rack so the air can circulate for 15 minutes before inverting onto the wire rack to cool completely.

6. To make the maple glaze, simply whisk together the icing sugar, butter, vanilla and maple syrup. Put a plate beneath the Bundt on the wire rack and pour over the glaze. Pour the glaze collected on the plate over the cake again to cover it entirely and scatter over the pumpkin seeds. This bundt will keep well in an airtight container for up to 5 days.

# Chocolate & Raspberry Cheesecake Bundt with Chocolate Ganache

I made my gooiest ever Raspberry Ripple Cheesecake Brownies with Perrie Edwards for the Little Mix YouTube channel and the recipe went viral, with the brownies being made all over the world, so this is the Bundt version of those brownies.

**For the 10-cup Bundt® pan:**
15g (1 tbsp/ ½oz) butter
15g (1 tbsp/ ½oz) plain flour

**For the cheesecake swirl:**
1 egg yolk
360g (1 ½ cups/12 ½oz) cream
   cheese
75g (¾ cup/2¾oz) icing sugar
150g (1 cup/5 ½oz) raspberries

**For the cake:**
75g (⅓ cup/2¾oz) cocoa
   powder
135g (1 cup/4¾oz) soft light
   brown sugar
175g (1 cup/6oz) golden
   caster sugar
50g (3 ½ tbsp/1¾oz) unsalted
   butter, softened
1 tsp vanilla bean paste
115ml (½ cup/3¾fl oz)
   boiling water
2 eggs
175ml (1 cup/6fl oz) soured
   cream
200g (1½ cups/7oz) plain flour
1 tsp baking powder
½ tsp bicarbonate of soda

**For the ganache:**
100g (½ cup/3 ½oz) semisweet
   chocolate
1 tbsp golden syrup
75ml (⅓ cup/2 ½fl oz) single
   cream

**To serve:**
Fresh raspberries
Vanilla ice cream

1. Preheat your oven to 160°C fan/180°C/350°F/gas 4.

2. Melt the butter , then use a pastry brush to brush it evenly over the inside of a 10-cup Bundt® pan, being careful to get into every nook and cranny. I find it easier to brush from the base up to prevent any butter pooling. Sift over the flour, moving the pan from side to side to coat it evenly. Turn it upside down and give it a final tap to remove any excess, then set aside.

3. Add the egg yolk, cream cheese and icing sugar to a medium bowl and whisk until smooth. Cover and refrigerate until ready to use.

4. To a large mixing bowl, add the cocoa powder, sugars, butter and vanilla. Pour over the boiling water and mix until smooth. Add the eggs and soured cream, mix again and then fold through the flour, baking powder and bicarbonate of soda. Mix until just combined. Pour two-thirds of the chocolate batter into the prepared pan and then add dollops of the cheesecake swirl followed by a few raspberries on top of each dollop, then pour the remaining batter over the top. Bake for 45–50 minutes. Leave to cool in the pan on a wire rack for 20 minutes and then invert onto the wire rack to cool completely.

5. To make the ganache, melt the chocolate, golden syrup and cream together in a small saucepan over a low heat. Pour over the Bundt. Fill the centre with raspberries and serve with vanilla ice cream.

# Chocolate & Malt Bundt with Chocolate Malted Frosting

This Bundt is a celebration of chocolate and malt. Malt can't help but impart a warm, fuzzy feeling of cosiness and the frosting actually tastes like the inside of a chocolate malt ball.

SERVES 12

**For the 12-cup Anniversary Bundt® pan:**

15g (1 tbsp/½oz) butter
15g (1 tbsp/½oz) cocoa powder

**For the cake:**

30g (2 tbsp/1oz) cocoa powder
50ml (¼ cup/2fl oz) boiling water
60ml (¼ cup/2fl oz) milk, hot
75g (½ cup/2¾oz) malt powder (I use Horlicks)
215g (2 sticks/7½oz) unsalted butter, softened
215g (1 cup/7½oz) caster sugar
1 tsp vanilla bean paste
4 eggs
215g (1¾ cups/7½oz) self-raising flour
1 tsp baking powder
125ml (½ cup/4fl oz) buttermilk

**For the malted frosting:**

125g (1 stick + 1 tbsp/4½oz) unsalted butter, softened
250g (1½ cups + 3 tbsp/9oz) icing sugar, sifted
50g (⅓ cup/1¾oz) malt powder
35ml (2 tbsp) soured cream

**To decorate:**

200g (2 cups/7oz) chocolate malt balls (I use Maltesers)

1. Preheat your oven to 160°C fan/180°C/350°F/gas 4.

2. Melt the butter, then use a pastry brush to brush it evenly over the inside of a 12-cup Anniversary Bundt® pan, being careful to get into every nook and cranny. I find it easier to brush from the base up to prevent any butter pooling. Sift over the cocoa powder, moving the pan from side to side to coat it evenly. Turn it upside down and give it a final tap to remove any excess, then set aside.

3. Put the cocoa powder in a small bowl or cup, pour over the boiling water and mix to a paste. In a separate bowl mix the hot milk with the malt powder and then set both aside to cool.

4. Place the butter and sugar in a large bowl and mix together using hand-held electric beaters. Add the vanilla and eggs, mix, and then add the flour and baking powder. Add a splash of buttermilk and you should have a dropping consistency. Divide the mixture in half and add the cocoa paste to one half and the malt paste to the other. Add large dollops of each batter alternately to the prepared pan and use a toothpick to swirl them together. Bake for 50–55 minutes or until a skewer inserted into the cake comes out clean. Leave to cool in the pan for 15 minutes and then invert onto a wire rack to cool completely.

5. To make the frosting, add the butter, icing sugar, malt powder and soured cream to the bowl of a stand mixer fitted with the whisk attachment and mix until smooth.

6. Spread the cooled Bundt generously with the frosting and then arrange Maltesers all over it in neat lines. This also makes a great celebration cake. This Bundt is best eaten on the day it's made but will keep in an airtight container for a few days.

# CHAPTER 6

# Jelly & Ice Cream

# Strawberry Trifle Bundt

———

I really had fun with this. A traditional trifle turned completely on its head
and I can't begin to explain the quiet thrill as you turn it out!

SERVES 8

**For the 10-cup Elegant
Party Bundt® pan:**
15g (1 tbsp/ ½oz) butter
15g (1 tbsp/ ½oz) plain flour

**For the cake:**
250g (2 stick+2 tbsp/9oz )
   unsalted butter, softened,
 250g (1 cup/9oz) caster sugar
1 tsp vanilla bean paste
4 eggs
250g (2 cups/9oz) self-raising
   flour

**For the jelly layer:**
Neutral-flavoured oil, for
   brushing
135g (4¾oz) strawberry jelly
650ml (3¼ cups/22fl oz)
   boiling water
8 strawberries, halved or
   quartered if large

1. Preheat your oven to 160°C fan/180°C/350°F/gas 4.

2. Melt the butter, then use a pastry brush to brush it evenly over
   the inside of a 10-cup Elegant Party Bundt® pan, being careful to
   get into every nook and cranny. I find it easier to brush from the
   base up to prevent any butter pooling. Sift over the flour, moving
   the pan from side to side to coat it evenly. Turn it upside down
   and give it a final tap to remove any excess, then set aside.

3. To make the sponge base, cream the butter and sugar together.
   Add the vanilla and eggs, beat until smooth and then fold the
   flour through. Pour the batter into the prepared Bundt® pan and
   bake for 40–45 minutes or until cooked through and a skewer
   inserted into the cake comes out clean. Leave to cool in the
   pan for 10 minutes and then invert onto a wire rack to cool
   completely. Once cool, slice the top off to create a flat surface
   for the trifle layers to sit on. Store in an airtight container while
   waiting for the remaining layers to come together.

4. Clean the Bundt® pan and brush lightly with oil. To make the
   jelly layer, melt the strawberry jelly in the boiling water. Pour it
   carefully into the pan and then place in your refrigerator. When
   the jelly is beginning to set, add the strawberries and leave to
   set in your refrigerator for at least 4 hours.

Ingredients and method continued overleaf →

**For the custard layer:**
4 platinum-grade gelatine
    leaves
300ml (1¼ cups/10fl oz)
    whole milk
4 egg yolks
75g (5 tbsp/⅓ cup/2¾oz)
    caster sugar
15g (1 tbsp/½oz) cornflour
60g (4 tbsp/2oz) custard
    powder
1 tsp vanilla bean paste
175ml (¾ cup/6¾fl oz)
    double cream

**To decorate:**
Whipped cream
Strawberries
Sprinkles (optional)

5. To make the custard layer, add the gelatine leaves to a bowl with cold water. Pour the milk into a saucepan and bring it to a simmer, without letting it boil, then remove from the heat. Add the egg yolks and caster sugar to a bowl and whisk them together. Add the cornflour, custard powder and vanilla and whisk until smooth, then gradually add the milk. When all the milk has been added, pour the custard into a clean saucepan. Heat over a medium heat and stir vigorously until the custard is smooth. Squeeze the water out of the gelatine leaves and add them to the custard. Place in a clean bowl and close cover with clingfilm so it doesn't form a skin. Refrigerate until ready to use.

6. Whip the double cream until firmly whipped (but not thick like butter). Fold it through the custard to create a creme diplomat and cover the jelly in the Bundt® pan with a thick layer. Smooth the top with a spatula and then refrigerate to set.

7. To serve, give the Bundt® pan a jiggle to loosen the jelly and custard and then place the sponge disc gently in the tin. Invert onto a serving plate. Fill the centre with whipped cream and strawberries, add sprinkles if desired and serve! This Bundt is best eaten on the day it's made.

# Summer Berry Pavlova Bundt

The recipe is really a semifreddo, meaning it's an easily put together form of ice cream. It's a very simple recipe and really allows you to enjoy the berry flavours you put into it.

**SERVES 8**

**For the berries:**
200g (1 ½ cups/7oz) mixture of fresh blueberries, raspberries, strawberries
50g (¼ cup/1 ¾oz) caster sugar
1 tsp vanilla bean paste

**For the ice cream:**
900ml (4 cups/1 ½ pints) double cream
4 egg whites
75g (⅓ cup/2 ¾oz) caster sugar
4 large meringue nests, broken into small pieces

**To decorate:**
150g (¾ cup/5 ½oz) mixed fresh berries
75g (1 cup/2 ¾oz) mini meringues
180g (1 cup/6oz) white chocolate, melted

1. Line a 10-cup Bundt® pan with clingfilm.

2. Place the berries, sugar and vanilla in a saucepan and heat until the berries collapse. Set aside to cool.

3. In a large mixing bowl, whip the double cream until stiff.

4. In a second large mixing bowl, beat the egg whites until almost stiff, then add the sugar and beat until you have a stiff, glossy meringue.

5. Gently fold the berries and whipped meringue into the whipped cream and then fold through the broken pieces of ready-made meringue. Pour into the prepared pan, smooth the surface and freeze for at least 4 hours or ideally overnight, if possible.

6. Remove the Bundt from the freezer and invert it onto a serving plate. Peel back the clingfilm. Decorate the top with berries, mini meringues and melted white chocolate. Although this is frozen, this type of ice cream tends to crystallise after a couple of days in the freezer, so ideally consume the same day it's made.

# Banana Split Ice-cream Bundt

A banana split is actually quite a simple dish but if those simple elements aren't all spot on it doesn't quite satisfy, so this hot chocolate fudge sauce recipe had to be everything!

SERVES 10

750ml (3 ¼ cups/1 ⅓ pints) chocolate ice cream
1 banana
750ml (3 ¼ cups/1 ⅓ pints) vanilla ice cream

**For the chocolate fudge sauce:**
75g (⅓ cup + 1 tbsp/2 ¾oz) soft light brown sugar
175g (½ cup/6oz) golden syrup
75ml (⅓ cup/2 ½fl oz) double cream
100g (⅓ cup/3 ½oz) sweetened condensed milk
180g (1 cup/6oz) dark chocolate
35g (2 tbsp/1 ¼oz) unsalted butter
A pinch of salt

**To decorate:**
50g (⅓ cup/1 ¾oz) hazelnuts, roasted and chopped
4 tbsp sprinkles
2 bananas, sliced
300ml (1 ½ cups/10fl oz) whipped cream
8 maraschino cherries

1. To make the fudge sauce, add the sugar, golden syrup, cream and condensed milk to a saucepan. Bring to a simmer and when it starts to bubble take it off the heat and add the chocolate, butter and salt. Leave to melt and then whisk until smooth. Pour into a jug and set aside until ready to use.

2. Line a 12-cup Original Bundt® pan with clingfilm.

3. Let the chocolate ice cream soften but not melt entirely, and then pour into the prepared pan. Use a spatula to level the surface. Peel and thinly slice the banana and lay the slices all over the surface. Spoon some of the chocolate fudge sauce over the banana slices, followed by a scattering of most of the chopped hazelnuts and sprinkles. Freeze for 30 minutes.

4. Remove the vanilla ice cream from the freezer and allow to soften but not melt entirely. Pour it over the bananas in the prepared pan and freeze again for at least 4 hours.

5. To serve, take the ice-cream Bundt out of the freezer and invert onto a serving plate. Arrange banana pieces on the top, surrounded by rosettes of whipped cream with maraschino cherries on them and sprinkle each rosette with chopped hazelnuts and sprinkles. Pour over hot fudge sauce at the last minute and serve. This Bundt needs to be eaten on the day it's turned out.

# Neapolitan Bundt Alaska with Popping Candy

This really is a retro showstopper and so easy to put together. Try to buy a naturally softer brand of ice cream and if you don't have time to make the sponge layer, then you can use shop-bought Madeira cake instead or leave it out all together!

SERVES 10

**For the ice-cream layers:**
750ml (3¼ cups/1⅓ pints) chocolate ice cream
750ml (3¼ cups/1⅓ pints) strawberry ice cream
750ml (3¼ cups/1⅓ pints) vanilla ice cream

**For the sponge layer:**
125g (1 stick + 1 tbsp/4½oz) unsalted butter
125g (½ cup/4½oz) caster sugar
2 eggs
1 tsp vanilla bean paste
125g (1 cup/4½oz) self-raising flour

1. Line a 10-cup Vintage Star Bundt® pan with clingfilm.

2. Remove the chocolate ice cream from the freezer and leave to soften, then mix with hand-held electric beaters until smooth. Pour into the prepared pan, smooth the top to be as level as possible and then freeze for 1–2 hours. Repeat with the strawberry and vanilla ice creams.

3. Preheat your oven to 160°C fan/180°C/350°F/gas 4 and line an oven tray with baking parchment.

4. To make the sponge, cream the butter and sugar together and then add the eggs and vanilla and mix to combine. Fold through the flour. Put the mixture into a piping bag (or freezer bag with a corner snipped off) and, starting in the centre of the prepared tray, pipe a spiral roughly the size of the base of your Bundt® pan. Bake for 15–20 minutes or until golden and a skewer inserted into the centre of the cake comes out clean. Peel back the parchment and leave to cool completely.

5. To make the Swiss meringue, place all the ingredients in a heatproof bowl over a pan of simmering water. Whisk continuously for around 5 minutes to dissolve the sugar and heat the egg whites. Once you can no longer feel sugar grains between your fingertips (taking care not to burn yourself), or the mixture reaches 80°C (176°F) on a sugar thermometer, remove from the heat and use hand-held electric beaters or a stand mixer to whisk until the mixture is very stiff and glossy.

**For the meringue:**
4 egg whites
400g (2 cups/14oz) caster
   sugar
1 tsp vanilla bean paste

**To serve:**
Popping candy

6. To assemble the Bundt Alaska, take the Bundt® pan out of the freezer. Place a plate on top of the sponge and cut around it so that it fits onto the ice cream. Use a cookie cutter to cut out the centre circle. Press the sponge on to the ice cream, then invert the Bundt onto a serving plate. Use a palette knife or piping bag to cover the whole Bundt in the meringue and then use a cook's blowtorch to gently brown it. Sprinkle the whole Bundt with popping candy and serve. Without the meringue the ice cream Bundt will freeze well for up to 3 months.

Images overleaf →

# Chocolate Charlotte Royale

There's perhaps no greater retro dish than this but sometimes the oldies are the goodies. It's quite effortless to make and yet still impresses as it arrives on the table, which makes it even more fabulous.

SERVES 6

1 x 26cm (10½in) chocolate
  Swiss roll

**For the mousse:**
125ml (½ cup/4floz) double
  cream
125g (¾ cup/4½oz) milk
  chocolate
125g (¾ cup/4½oz) dark
  chocolate
4 eggs, separated
50g (¼ cup/1¾oz) golden
  caster sugar

**To serve:**
Whipped cream

1. Line a 10-cup Bundt® pan with clingfilm. You will need 2 pieces so you can line all the way up the sides and centre. Take the Swiss roll and slice it into 1cm (½in)-thick pieces and then arrange them so they cover the entire pan. If there are any gaps, cut small pieces of Swiss roll to fill them.

2. To make the mousse, add the double cream and both chocolates to a saucepan and heat very gently to melt them together.

3. Put the egg whites into a large bowl and whisk them until stiff peaks form, then towards the end, add the sugar.

4. Remove the melted chocolate from the heat and beat in the egg yolks until smooth. Add a spoonful of this mixture to the egg whites and use a metal spoon fold it through, then add the remaining mixture, folding gently to retain the air. Pour the mousse into the prepared pan. Place pieces of Swiss roll all over the top of the chocolate mousse, cover in clingfilm and refrigerate for at least 5 hours or ideally overnight, if possible.

5. Place a plate on top of the Bundt® pan and then invert your Chocolate Charlotte Royale onto it. Remove the clingfilm and serve with whipped cream. This Bundt will keep in a refrigerator for a couple of days.

# Raspberry Charlotte Royale

The raspberry sister of the Chocolate Royale (opposite) and
she's also very pretty! Serve with retro pride after prawn cocktails
and chicken Kievs.

SERVES 6

1 x 26cm (10½in) raspberry
   Swiss roll

**For the mousse:**
2 gelatine leaves
270g (2½ cups/9¾oz) fresh
   raspberries
100g (½ cup/3½oz) golden
   caster sugar
400ml (1¾ cups/14fl oz)
   double cream

1. Line a 10-cup Bundt® pan with clingfilm. Slice the Swiss roll into slim slices (1cm or ½in thick) and arrange them in the pan so the interior is entirely covered. If there are any gaps, cut small pieces of Swiss roll to fill them.

2. To make the raspberry mousse, place the gelatine leaves in a bowl of cold water.

3. Add 150g (1½ cups/5½oz) raspberries to a small saucepan and pour over the sugar. Heat until juicy and soft.

4. Whip the double cream until almost stiffly whipped, so it still retains some softness. Set aside.

5. Pass the raspberries through a sieve and back into the saucepan. Take the gelatine leaves out of the water, give them a squeeze to get rid of any excess water, then add them to the saucepan. Heat over a medium heat and mix for a few minutes until smooth. Pour the raspberries over the whipped cream and mix in. Fold through the remaining whole raspberries at the end and spoon into the Bundt® pan on top of the Swiss roll slices. Top the mousse with slices of Swiss roll, then cover with clingfilm. Refrigerate for at least 5 hours or ideally overnight, if possible.

6. Place a plate on top of the Bundt® pan and then invert your raspberry Royale on to it. Remove the clingfilm and serve. This Bundt will keep for a couple of days when refrigerated.

# Triple Chocolate Cheesecake Bundt

This one has to be made in three stages to achieve the very defined layers of chocolate but it's all quite simple and the result is a rich, set, triple chocolate mousse that is absolutely worth it. You can serve quite delicate slices as the richness will satisfy the keenest of chocoholics.

SERVES 8

**For the 5-cup Lotus Bundt® pan:**
Vegetable oil

**For the white chocolate layer:**
1 platinum-grade gelatine leaves
100ml (¼ cup + 3 tbsp/4fl oz) double cream
65g (¼ cup + 1tbsp/2½oz) cream cheese
65g (¼ cup + 1tbsp/2½oz) mascarpone
25g (2 tbsp + 2tsp/1oz) icing sugar
¼ tsp vanilla bean paste
75g (¼ cup + 3 tbsp/3oz) white chocolate, melted

**For the milk chocolate layer:**
1 platinum-grade gelatine leaves
100ml (¼ cup + 3 tbsp/4fl oz) double cream
65g (¼ cup + 1tbsp/2½oz) cream cheese
65g (¼ cup + 1tbsp/2½oz) mascarpone
25g (2 tbsp + 2tsp/1oz) icing sugar
¼ tsp vanilla bean paste
75g (¼ cup + 3 tbsp/3oz) milk chocolate, melted

**For the dark chocolate layer:**
1 platinum grade-gelatine leaves
100ml (¼ cup + 3 tbsp/4fl oz) double cream
65g (¼ cup + 1tbsp/2½oz) cream cheese
65g (¼ cup + 1tbsp/2½oz) mascarpone
25g (2 tbsp + 2tsp/1oz) icing sugar
¼ tsp vanilla bean paste
75g (¼ cup + 3 tbsp/3oz) dark chocolate, melted

Method overleaf →

1. Brush a 5-cup Lotus Bundt® pan with vegetable oil.

2. To make the white chocolate layer, put the gelatine leaves in a bowl, cover with cold water and leave to soak. Heat the double cream gently in a small saucepan. Take a mixing bowl and beat the cream cheese, mascarpone, icing sugar and vanilla together. Remove the cream from the heat, squeeze out the gelatine leaves and add them to the cream. Use a whisk to mix them in. Pour the cream on to the cream cheese and mascarpone and beat it all together. Add the melted white chocolate, mix until smooth then pour into the prepared pan. Refrigerate for a few hours until fully set.

3. To make the milk chocolate layer, repeat the step above but with the melted milk chocolate.

4. To make the dark chocolate layer, repeat the step above but with the melted dark chocolate.

5. Bash the cookies in a pestle and mortar or in a freezer bag with a rolling pin and then place in a bowl with the melted butter. Remove the cheesecake from the refrigerator and spoon the cookies over the top, pressing them very gently in. Return to the refrigerator to set fully, for at least 4 hours but ideally overnight, if possible.

6. Invert the Bundt® pan onto a serving plate. If the cheesecake doesn't just slip out, stand the pan in hot water for 10 seconds to loosen it. Decorate the top with white, milk and dark chocolate curls and serve. This Bundt could be made in advance as it will keep for a few days when refrigerated.

# Mascarpone, Cherry & Pistachio Ice-cream Bundt with Hard Chocolate Shell

I'm an eighties child, from a time of Soda Streams and Cabbage Patch Kids when you could buy Ice Magik, a pouring chocolate that hardens and creates a chocolate shell just as it hits your ice cream. What I didn't know then was that all you have to do is add coconut oil to chocolate and it works, just like magic.

SERVES 8

250g (1 cup/9oz) fresh cherries
100g (½ cup/3½oz) caster sugar
1 tbsp cornflour
600ml (2 ⅔ cups/20fl oz) double cream
600g (3 cups/1lb 5oz) mascarpone
1 x 397g (1 cup/14oz) can sweetened condensed milk
200g (12 biscuits/7oz) digestive biscuits
50g (½ cup/1¾oz) chopped pistachios
¼ tsp almond extract
50g (3½ tbsp/1¾oz) unsalted butter, melted

**For the chocolate shell:**
225g (1¼ cups/8oz) milk or dark chocolate
1 tbsp coconut oil

**To decorate:**
50g (½ cup/1¾oz) pistachios, chopped
250g (1 cup/9oz) fresh cherries

1. Line a 10-cup Bundt® pan with clingfilm.

2. Remove the stones from the cherries and add them to a saucepan with the sugar. Simmer until juicy but still holding their shape. Drain the cherries, reserving the liquid, and then return the liquid to the saucepan over a high heat for a few minutes to reduce and become syrupy so the cherry flavour is intensified. Make a paste in a separate bowl from a splash of cold water and the cornflour. Pour it into the saucepan and heat briefly again to thicken further and then set aside to cool.

3. Whip the double cream until stiff with hand-held electric beaters and fold the mascarpone and condensed milk through and then briefly swirl the cherries in. Pour into the prepared pan and smooth over the surface with a spatula. Freeze for 30 minutes.

4. Crush the digestive biscuits and mix with the chopped pistachios. Pour the almond extract and melted butter on to them and mix together. Remove the Bundt from the freezer and press the crushed biscuits into the ice cream, then freeze again for at least 4 hours.

5. To finish the Bundt, lift the ice cream out of the Bundt® pan and place on a serving plate. To make the chocolate shell, melt the chocolate and coconut oil together in a heatproof bowl in the microwave in 30-second bursts. Pour over the top of the Bundt and, before it sets, scatter over the chopped pistachios. Fill the centre with a pile of fresh cherries and serve.

# Chocolate, Peanut Butter & Caramel Ice-cream Bundt with Salted Pretzels

---

If indulgence is what you're after, then this is the Bundt for you.
Think sticky, chocolate, salted caramel heaven (but you might need
to go for a walk afterwards).

SERVES 10

750ml (3¼ cups/1⅓ pints) vanilla ice cream

750ml (3¼ cups/1⅓ pints) chocolate ice cream

300g (1 cup/10½oz) chocolate fudge sauce (see page 138 or use shop-bought)

300g (1⅓ cups/10½oz) caramel sauce (see page 236 or use shop-bought)

150g (2 cups/5½oz) mini marshmallows

100g (1 cup/3½oz) mini salted pretzels

200g (12 biscuits/7oz) chocolate digestive biscuits

60g (½ stick/2¼oz) unsalted butter, melted

75g (½ cup/2¾oz) salted peanuts

1. Line a 12-cup Anniversary Braided Bundt® pan with clingfilm.

2. Let both ice creams soften but not melt entirely and then pour the vanilla ice cream into the prepared pan. Smooth the top with a spatula to make it level. Drizzle over half the chocolate fudge sauce, half the caramel sauce and scatter over half the marshmallows and salted pretzels. Pour over the softened chocolate ice cream and smooth the surface out so it is as level as possible. Freeze for 30 minutes.

3. Put the chocolate digestive biscuits into a freezer bag and bash them into crumbs. Add the melted butter to them. Spoon over the ice cream and gently press them in to form a base. Put the ice-cream Bundt back into the freezer and freeze for at least 5 hours but ideally overnight.

4. When ready to serve, invert the ice-cream Bundt onto a serving plate. Drizzle over the remaining chocolate fudge sauce and caramel sauce and scatter over the remaining marshmallows and the peanuts. Arrange the remaining salted pretzels all over the sides and then serve. This Bundt can be kept frozen without the toppings for up to 2 months.

# Blueberry & Lemon Layered Crème Fraîche Bundt

This Bundt is so simple to put together and looks rather elegant
for a summer lunch party.

SERVES 8

300g (2 cups/10½oz) fresh
   blueberries
75g (⅓ cup/2¾oz) caster
   sugar
Juice of 1 lemon
900ml (4 cups/1½ pints)
   double cream
200g (1¾ cups/7oz) icing
   sugar
900ml (3¾ cups/1½ pints)
   crème fraîche
360g (1¼ cups/12½oz) lemon
   curd
200g (12 biscuits/7oz)
   digestive biscuits, crushed

**To decorate:**
100g (¾ cup/3½oz) fresh
   blueberries
2 lemons, thinly sliced
A selection of edible flowers

1. Line a 10-cup Bundt® pan with clingfilm.

2. Place the blueberries, sugar and lemon juice in a small saucepan and heat until juicy and the blueberries lose their shape. Remove from the heat and leave to cool.

3. Whip the cream with the icing sugar until stiff peaks form and then fold though the crème fraîche. Add one-third of the mixture to the prepared pan, smooth with a spatula to level it out and then add half the blueberries, dollops of half the lemon curd and sprinkle over half the crushed biscuits. Add another third of the ice cream and repeat with the remaining blueberries, lemon curd and biscuits. End with a last layer of cream mixture and freeze for at least 4 hours or ideally overnight.

4. Remove the Bundt from the freezer and invert it onto a serving plate. Add the blueberries, lemon slices and edible flowers to decorate. This Bundt will keep for a couple of days in the freezer, but may crystallise if left too much longer.

# Cocoa Panna Cotta with Funfetti & Chocolate Chip Shortbread

Chocolate panna cotta is simply heavenly, and to keep the tone fun the funfetti found its way into the accompanying shortbread.

MAKES 6

**For the Brilliance Bundtlette Bundt® pan:**
Vegetable oil, for greasing

**For the cocoa panna cotta:**
7 gelatine leaves
1 tsp vanilla bean paste
600ml (2 ⅔ cups/20fl oz) double cream
100g (¾ cup/3 ½oz) cocoa powder
400ml (2 cups/14fl oz) whole milk
75g (⅓ cup/2¾oz) caster sugar

**For the funfetti and chocolate chip shortbread:**
220g (2 sticks/8oz) butter
A pinch of salt
175g (1⅓ cups/6oz) icing sugar
1 tsp vanilla bean paste
375g (3 cups/13oz) plain flour
2 eggs
100g (¾ cup/3½oz) dark or milk chocolate chips
4 tbsp funfetti sprinkles

**To decorate:**
150g (1¼ cups/5½oz) fresh raspberries

1. Brush each hole of a Brilliance Bundtlette Bundt® pan with vegetable oil.

2. Put the gelatine leaves in a bowl of cold water and leave them to soften.

3. Add the vanilla, double cream, cocoa powder, milk and sugar to a saucepan. Bring to a gentle simmer, then remove from the heat. Squeeze the water out of the gelatine leaves and whisk them into the cream. Whisk until fully dissolved and then transfer the mixture to a jug, passing through a fine-mesh sieve. Pour into the prepared pan and refrigerate for 1–2 hours until set.

4. To make the shortbread, beat the butter, salt and icing sugar together until pale and fluffy. Add the eggs and beat slowly until combined. Then add the vanilla and flour and beat again until combined. Add the chocolate chips and funfetti and mix again so they're evenly distributed. Place in clingfilm and roll it up into a log. Refrigerate for at least 5 hours or ideally overnight, if possible.

5. Preheat your oven to 180°C fan/200°C/400°F/gas 6.

6. Remove the dough from the refrigerator and cut into thick slices (1.5cm/⅝in). Place them on a baking tray and bake for 10–12 minutes. Remove from the oven and leave to cool on the tray.

7. Carefully invert the cocoa panna cotta onto a board and transfer them to serving plates. Fill the centres with raspberries and serve with the shortbread on the side. The panna cottas can be made a day ahead and kept refrigerated. The shortbread can also be made ahead of time and stored in an airtight container.

# Vanilla Panna Cotta with Rhubarb & Rose & a Sable Biscuit

Panna cotta mini Bundts look like something made by a pastry chef. They are so delicate and pretty and their appearance is only enhanced by the blush pink of the rhubarb and fluted edge of the sablé biscuits. If you don't have time to make the biscuits, you can use shop-bought shortbread instead.

MAKES 6

**For the Brilliance Bundtlette® Pan:**
Vegetable oil

**For the panna cotta:**
7 platinum-grade gelatine leaves
1 tsp vanilla bean paste
600ml (2⅔ cups/20fl oz) double cream
400ml (2 cups/14fl oz) whole milk
75g (⅓ cup/2.5oz) caster sugar
¼ tsp rose water

**For the sablé biscuits:**
220g (2 sticks/8oz) unsalted butter, chilled
A pinch of salt
220g (2 cups/8oz) caster sugar
½ tsp vanilla bean paste
370g (4 cups/13oz) plain flour
2 eggs

**For the rhubarb:**
300g (3 cups/10½oz) rhubarb
50g (½ cup/1¾oz) caster sugar

**To decorate:**
Edible rose petals (optional)

1. Brush each hole of the Brilliance Bundlette® pan with vegetable oil.

2. Put the gelatine leaves in a bowl of cold water and leave to soften.

3. Add the vanilla, double cream, milk, sugar and rose water to a saucepan. Bring to a gentle simmer, then remove from the heat. Squeeze the water out of the gelatine leaves and whisk them into the cream. Whisk until fully dissolved and then transfer to a jug, passing through a fine-mesh sieve. Pour into the prepared pan. Refrigerate for 1–2 hours until set.

4. To make the biscuits, cream the butter, salt, sugar, vanilla and flour together in a blender (for best results) until the mixture resembles breadcrumbs. Add the eggs and mix together to form a dough. Wrap in clingfilm and refrigerate for at least 1 hour. Remove from the freezer, then roll out and cut 6 circles just larger than the mini Bundts. Chill again for 1 hour.

5. Preheat your oven to 180°C fan/200°C/400°F/gas 6.

6. Place the biscuits on a baking sheet and bake for 8–10 minutes. Remove from the oven and leave to cool on the tray.

7. To prepare the rhubarb, trim the ends off and cut into 1cm pieces. Toss them in the sugar and then put them in an ovenproof dish, cover with foil and roast for 15 minutes.

8. To assemble, place the rose panna cotta on plates with the shortbread and roast rhubarb (warm or cold). Decorate with a few rose petals if desired and serve. The panna cottas, rhubarb and shortbread can all be made a couple of days in advance and then assembled at the time of serving.

# Chocolate, Hazelnut, Caramel & Marshmallow Semifreddo

This is one of those recipes that appeals to both young and old.
My daughter steals spoonfuls out of the freezer while it's setting
and my mother goes back for seconds too.

**SERVES 8**

**For the ice cream:**
900ml (4 cups/1½ pints)
    double cream
4 egg whites
75g (⅓ cup/2¾oz) caster sugar

**For the swirl:**
200g (¾ cup + 2 tbsp/7oz)
    caramel, either shop-bought
    or use caramel recipe from
    the New Year's Eve Bundt
    (page 236)
200g (¾ cup/7oz) chocolate
    hazelnut spread (I use Nutella)
50g (½ cup/1¾oz) roasted
    hazelnuts, chopped

**For the marshmallow
    (optional):**
2 egg whites
200g (1 cup/7oz) caster sugar
½ tsp vanilla bean paste
A pinch of salt

**To decorate:**
50g (¼ cup/1¾oz) caramel,
    warmed
50g (½ cup/1¾oz) chocolate
    hazelnut spread, warmed
50g (½ cup/1¾oz) roasted
    hazelnuts

1. Line a 10-cup Bundt® pan with clingfilm.

2. Take 2 large mixing bowls. Add the double cream to one and whip it until softly whipped but holding its shape. Add the egg whites to the other bowl and beat until white and frothy, then add the sugar and continue to beat until stiff and glossy.

3. Warm the caramel in a microwave or saucepan to soften it. Fold the chocolate hazelnut spread and chopped hazelnuts through it.

4. Fold the cream, egg whites and caramel mixture together. It doesn't need to be entirely smooth and the caramel should be swirled through it rather than blended, and then gently fold through the hazelnuts. Spoon into the prepared pan, smooth the top with a spatula and freeze for at least 4 hours or ideally overnight.

5. If you want to make the marshmallow, place all the ingredients in a heatproof bowl over a pan of simmering water (making sure the bowl doesn't touch the water). Whisk continuously for around 5 minutes to dissolve the sugar and heat the egg whites. Once you can no longer feel sugar grains between your fingertips (taking care not to burn yourself), or the mixture reaches 80°C (176°F) on a sugar thermometer, remove from the heat and use hand-held electric beaters or a stand mixer to whisk until the mixture is very stiff and glossy.

6. Remove the Bundt® pan from the freezer and invert it onto a serving plate. Use a palette knife or piping bag to cover the top of the Bundt with the marshmallow, if using, and then use a cook's blowtorch to gently brown it. Drizzle over the warm caramel, warm chocolate, add the hazelnuts and hazelnut spread to serve.

# Elderflower Panna Cotta with Champagne Jelly & Edible Flowers

Pretty. Pretty. Pretty. This is such a gorgeous grown-up take on jelly and custard!

SERVES 8

**For the 10-cup Bundt® pan:**
Cake release spray (see page 240 for homemade) or vegetable oil

**For the champagne jelly:**
4 platinum-grade gelatine leaves
400ml (1¾ cups/14fl oz) champagne, prosecco or sparkling wine
200ml (1 cup/7fl oz) water
50g (¼ cup/1¾oz) caster sugar
8 edible flowers, such as violas, pansies, cornflowers

**For the panna cotta:**
7 platinum-grade gelatine leaves
1 tsp vanilla bean paste
200ml (1 cup/14fl oz) whole milk
75g (⅓ cup/2¾oz) caster sugar
4 tbsp elderflower cordial
800ml (3½ cups/1⅓ pints) double cream

**To decorate:**
Extra edible flowers
Raspberries

1. Spray a 10-cup Bundt® pan with cake release spray or brush it with vegetable oil.

2. Put the gelatine leaves in a bowl with the champagne (or prosecco or sparkling wine) and leave to soften.

3. Heat the water and sugar together in a saucepan to dissolve the sugar, then heat until simmering. Squeeze out the gelatine leaves, add them to the saucepan and whisk continuously until they're fully dissolved. Pass the mixture through a fine-mesh sieve into the champagne and then whisk everything together. Pour into the prepared pan and chill in the refrigerator. When it starts to thicken – after about 20 minutes – add the edible flowers, facing downwards, and return to the refrigerator to set.

4. Put the gelatine leaves for the panna cotta into a bowl of cold water. If you used vegetable oil to grease the Bundt® pan, remove the set jelly from the pan, brush the pan with vegetable oil again and return the jelly to the pan.

5. Add the vanilla, milk, sugar and elderflower cordial to a saucepan. Bring to a gentle simmer and then remove from the heat. Squeeze the water out of the gelatine leaves and whisk them into the cream. Whisk until fully dissolved and then transfer to a jug, passing through a fine-mesh sieve, and pour gently onto the set jelly. Refrigerate for about 4 hours until set, but ideally leave it overnight, if possible.

6. Carefully invert the jelly and panna cotta onto a serving plate. Decorate with extra edible flowers and raspberries and serve. I find jellies are best. This Bundt is best eaten on the day it is made.

# CHAPTER 7

# Bun Bundts

# Bun Bundts

These buns are the ultimate in squishy, pull-apart rolls of sweet deliciousness. I love that they're easy to make and within 2 hours you can have buns on the table to rival any patisserie. I've shared a basic recipe and then a choice of variations but this is one to be creative with – dress them up, dress them down, try out your favourite flavours, no matter how outrageous they may seem, and make them your own.

MAKES 8

250ml (1¼ cups/9fl oz) whole milk, warmed
65g (½ stick/2¼oz) unsalted butter, plus extra for greasing
2 eggs, plus 1 egg, beaten
85g (⅓ cup/3oz) caster sugar
1 tsp sea salt
300g (1¾ cups/10½oz) strong bread flour
7g (1½ tsp/1 sachet) fast-action dried yeast
200g (1¼ cups/7oz) plain flour
Filling of your choice (see pages 161–169)

1. Put the milk and butter in a saucepan and heat gently to melt the butter and warm the milk, but don't let it boil.

2. Take the bowl from a stand mixer, add the eggs and sugar and whisk them together. Add the salt and then pour in the warm milk and butter. Add the strong flour, sprinkle over the yeast, and then add the plain flour. Place under the stand mixer fitted with the dough hook and knead for 10 minutes.

3. Place the dough in a lightly oiled bowl, cover with clingfilm and leave somewhere warm for about an hour until doubled in size.

4. Preheat your oven to 160°C fan/180°C/350°F/gas 4 and butter a 12-cup Bundt® pan.

5. Roll out the dough into a large rectangle measuring 60 x 40cm (24 x 16in). Add your choice of filling and then roll up the rectangle from the long side to make a long roll. Cut the roll into 8 even-sized pieces and then arrange them in the prepared pan with their spiralled edges pointing upwards. Brush with the beaten egg. Bake for 35–40 minutes. If they start to brown too much on top, simply cover with foil. Leave to cool in the pan for 10 minutes and then remove to a wire rack to cool completely. These are best eaten on the day they're made but could be enjoyed the following day if gently warmed in a low oven.

# Classic Cinnamon Buns

———

Always a classic and absolutely deservedly so!

MAKES 8

Butter, for greasing
Bun Bundt dough (opposite)
1 egg, beaten

**For the filling:**
120g (½ cup/4¼oz) light
   muscovado sugar
2 tbsp ground cinnamon

**For the cinnamon milk glaze:**
115g (1 cup/4oz) icing sugar
1 tbsp ground cinnamon
½ tsp vanilla bean paste
4 tbsp whole milk

**To finish:**
2 tbsp demerara sugar

1. Preheat your oven to 160°C fan/180°C/350°F/gas 4 and butter a 12-cup Anniverary Bundt® pan.

2. Roll out the dough into a large rectangle measuring 60 x 40cm (24 x 16in) and sprinkle over the sugar and cinnamon.

3. Roll up the rectangle from the long side to make a long roll. Cut the roll into 8 even-sized pieces and arrange them in the prepared pan with their spiralled edges pointing upwards. Brush with the beaten egg. Bake for 35–40 minutes. If they start to brown too much on top, simply cover with foil. Leave to cool in the pan for 10 minutes and then remove to a wire rack to cool completely.

4. To make the glaze, whisk the icing sugar, cinnamon and vanilla together and then add the milk little-by-little until you just reach a pouring consistency. Drizzle the glaze over the buns, then sprinkle the demerara sugar over the top and serve. These are best eaten on the day they're made or gently warmed on the second day.

# Blueberry Cheesecake Buns with Blueberry Glaze

The blueberry glaze on this Bundt is the most magnificent shade of bright purple which can't help but delight.

MAKES 8

Butter, for greasing
Bun Bundt dough (page 160)
1 egg, beaten

**For the filling:**
225g (1¾ cups/8oz) cream
   cheese, room temperature
100g (½ cup/3½oz) golden
   caster sugar
200g (2 cups/7oz) fresh
   blueberries

**For the blueberry glaze:**
115g (1 cup/4oz) icing sugar
100g (⅓ cup/3½oz) fresh
   blueberries

1. Preheat your oven to 160°C fan/180°C/350°F/gas 4 and butter a 12-cup Anniversary Bundt® pan.

2. Roll out the dough into a large rectangle measuring 60 x 40cm (24 x 16in) and spread with the cream cheese, right up to the edges. I find using an offset spatula is the easiest way to do this. Sprinkle over the sugar and then evenly scatter over the blueberries.

3. Roll up the rectangle from the long side to make a long roll. Cut the roll into 8 even-sized pieces, then arrange them in the prepared pan with their spiralled edges pointing upwards. Brush with the beaten egg. Bake for 35–40 minutes. If they start to brown too much on top, simply cover with foil. Leave to cool in the pan for 10 minutes and then remove to a wire rack to cool completely.

4. To make the glaze, simply add the sugar and blueberries to a blender and then drizzle the sauce over the buns. To change the consistency to your liking, simply add more icing sugar or more blueberries. These are best eaten the day they're made – make the glaze just before serving to retain the bright colour.

# Gingerbread Buns

These are autumn buns and should be made at around the same time the coffee shops start selling their pumpkin-spiced lattes.

MAKES 8

Butter, for greasing
Bun Bundt dough (page 160)
1 egg, beaten

**For the filling:**
2 tbsp ground ginger
1 tbsp ground cinnamon
120g (½ cup/4¼oz) light
    muscovado sugar
75g (¾ cup/2¾oz) preserved
    ginger in syrup

**For the ginger milk glaze:**
115g (1 cup/4oz) icing sugar
3 tbsp preserved ginger syrup
2 tbsp whole milk, plus extra
    to loosen (optional)
1 tsp vanilla bean paste

1. Preheat your oven to 160°C fan/180°C/350°F/gas 4 and butter a 12-cup Anniversary Bundt® pan.

2. Roll out the dough into a large rectangle measuring 60 x 40cm (24 x 16in) and sprinkle over the ground ginger, cinnamon and sugar. Grate the preserved ginger, reserving the syrup for the glaze, and scatter that over too.

3. Roll up the rectangle from the long side to make a long roll. Cut the roll into 8 even-sized pieces, then arrange them in the prepared pan with their spiralled edges pointing upwards. Brush with the beaten egg. Bake for 35–40 minutes. If they start to brown too much on top, simply cover with foil. Leave to cool in the pan for 10 minutes and then remove to a wire rack to cool completely.

4. To make the glaze, whisk the icing sugar, ginger syrup, milk and vanilla together. Add extra milk, a teaspoon at a time, if you prefer a looser consistency. Drizzle over the buns and serve. These are best enjoyed warm on the day they're made.

# Jelly Doughnut Buns

Jelly. Doughnut. Buns. No more words necessary.

MAKES 8

Butter, for greasing
Bun Bundt dough (page 160)
1 egg, beaten

**For the filling:**
150g (½ cup/5½oz) seedless
  raspberry jam
125g (1 cup/4½oz) fresh
  raspberries
120g (½ cup/4¼oz) caster
  sugar

**For the raspberry milk glaze:**
120g (1 cup/4¼oz) icing sugar
1 tsp seedless raspberry jam
3 tbsp whole milk

**To decorate:**
2 tbsp freeze-dried raspberry
  pieces

1. Preheat your oven to 160°C fan/180°C/350°F/gas 4 and butter a 12-cup Anniversary Bundt® pan.

2. Roll out the dough into a large rectangle measuring 60 x 40cm (24 x 16in) and spread the jam thinly over it. Scatter over the raspberries and then sprinkle with the sugar.

3. Roll up the rectangle from the long side to make a long roll. Cut the roll into 8 even-sized pieces, then arrange them in the prepared pan with their spiralled edges pointing upwards. Brush with the beaten egg. Bake for 35–40 minutes. If they start to brown too much on top, simply cover with foil. Leave to cool in the pan for 10 minutes and then remove to a wire rack to cool completely.

4. To make the glaze, whisk all the ingredients together, adding enough milk to create a pourable glaze. Drizzle over the Bundt and sprinkle over the freeze-dried raspberries to decorate. These buns are best eaten on the day they're made, but could be gently warmed in the oven the next day.

# Stickiest Salted Caramel Fig & Walnut Buns

Sticky buns will always be good for the soul, especially when your kitchen smells like a fairground from the caramel.

MAKES 8

Butter, for greasing
Bun Bundt dough (page 160)
1 egg, beaten

**For the filling:**
110g (1 stick/4oz) unsalted butter, room temperature
120g (½ cup/4¼oz) light muscovado sugar
200g (2 cups/7oz) soft dried figs
75g (½ cup/2¾oz) walnuts

**For the glaze:**
40g (⅓ stick/1¼oz) unsalted butter
120g (1 cup/4¼oz) icing sugar
1 tsp vanilla bean paste
½ tsp sea salt
Milk (optional)

**To serve:**
50g walnuts, chopped
Fresh figs

1. Preheat your oven to 160°C fan/180°C/350°F/gas 4 and butter a 12-cup Anniversary Bundt® pan.

2. Roll out the dough into a large rectangle measuring 60 x 40cm (24 x 16in) and spread the butter thinly over the top, then sprinkle over the sugar. Roughly chop the figs and walnuts and scatter them over the top.

3. Roll up the rectangle from the long side to make a long roll. Cut the roll into 8 even-sized pieces, then arrange them in the prepared pan with their spiralled edges pointing upwards. Brush with the beaten egg. Bake for 35–40 minutes. If they start to brown too much on top, simply cover with foil. Leave to cool in the pan for 10 minutes and then remove to a wire rack to cool completely.

4. To make the glaze, add the butter to a small pan and melt it over a low heat, then continue to heat until it browns but doesn't burn. Pour through a fine-mesh sieve (the browned butter gets little brown flecks in it) onto the icing sugar. Stir in the vanilla and salt and whisk until smooth (add milk if needed to loosen). Pour over the buns, scatter over some chopped walnuts and serve with a few fresh figs on the side. These buns are best eaten on the day they're made and ideally while still warm from the oven.

# Hazelnut & Almond
# Praline Buns

———————

Praline paste is chocolate hazelnut spread's cousin and if you two haven't met before I'm really excited to introduce you. It seems only fair to warn you that this nutty caramel paste tastes so good that you will be eating it by the spoonful. I've shared my recipe for making it from scratch but you can also buy it ready-made. It's great for using in other bakes, too, from praline-flavoured cheesecake to praline whipped cream for choux buns.

MAKES 8

Butter, for greasing
Bun Bundt dough (page 160)
1 egg, beaten

**For the praline paste:**
100g (⅔ cup/3½oz) blanched
　　hazelnuts
100g (⅔ cup/3½oz) blanched
　　almonds
100g (½ cup/3½oz) caster
　　sugar
45ml (3 tbsp/1½fl oz) water
2 tsp sea salt
150ml (⅔ cup/5fl oz) single
　　cream
2 tbsp vegetable oil

**For the glaze:**
2 tbsp praline paste
120g (½ cup/4¼oz) icing
　　sugar
2 tbsp whole milk, plus extra
　　to loosen (optional)
1 tbsp melted butter

1. Preheat your oven to 160°C fan/180°C/350°F/gas 4 and butter a 12-cup Anniversary Bundt® pan.

2. Place the nuts on a baking tray and roast for 5 minutes. You just want them lightly roasted so they release their flavour. Set aside to cool.

3. Add the sugar and water to a saucepan. Heat gently at first to dissolve the sugar, then increase the heat and, without stirring, watch as it turns a dark amber – this will take about 5 minutes. If you get a dark amber patch, simply give the saucepan a swirl and the dark patch will dilute and spread – at that point it's ready. Have a baking sheet lined with baking parchment beside you (or a silicone mat), then pour the caramel on to it. Leave to set for around 10 minutes at room temperature or until hard.

4. Break up the cooled caramel and place in a blender with the roasted nuts and salt. Blend together – at first, they'll be powdery, but then will quickly turn into a paste as the oils are released from the nuts. Pour in the cream and oil and blend until smooth. Spoon into a jar and your praline paste is ready to use. Keep refrigerated.

5. Roll out the dough into a large rectangle measuring 60 x 40cm (24 x 16in) and spread it with most of the praline paste, reserving 2 tablespoons for the glaze.

6. Roll up the rectangle from the long side to make a long roll. Cut the roll into 8 even-sized pieces, then arrange them in the prepared pan with their spiralled edges pointing upwards. Brush with the beaten egg. Bake for 35–40 minutes. If they start to brown too much on top, simply cover with foil. Leave to cool in the pan for 10 minutes and then remove to a wire rack to cool completely.

7. To make the glaze, whisk the remaining praline paste, icing sugar, milk and butter together. Add extra milk, a teaspoon at a time, if you prefer a looser consistency. Drizzle over the buns and serve. These are best eaten on the day they're made.

# Happy Buns

MAKES 8

Butter, for greasing
Bun Bundt dough (page 160)
1 egg, beaten

**For the filling:**
225g (1¾ cups/8oz) cream cheese
120g (½ cup/4¼oz) caster sugar
4 tbsp 100's & 1000's

**For the glaze:**
125g (½ cup/4½oz) cream cheese
125g (½ cup/4½oz) icing sugar
½ tsp vanilla bean paste
4 tbsp milk

**To finish:**
2 tbsp hundreds and thousands

Proving that these buns truly can be dressed for any occasion, these happy buns add a little fun to even the darkest day!

1. Once the dough has been rolled out to a rectangle measuring 60 x 40cm (24 x 16in), spread it with the cream cheese. Sprinkle over the sugar and then the hundreds and thousands. Follow the instructions from point 6 of the main recipe, above.

2. To make the glaze, whisk together the cream cheese, icing sugar and vanilla, then add the milk little by little until you just reach a pouring consistency. Pour over the buns, then sprinkle the hundreds and thousands over.

# CHAPTER 8

# Bread, Babka & Bundtnuts

# Hot Cross Bundt

———

I love the way the word Bundt fits so harmoniously with so many recipe names, as in this for a Hot Cross Bundt (another example of a similar joy was naming the Bundt Alaska on page 140). You get a whole loaf to slice, share and toast the next day and it makes a perfect Easter gift if you fill the centre with mini chocolate eggs and wrap it in cellophane with a pastel-coloured bow.

SERVES 8

**For the 12-cup Bundt® pan:**
Butter, melted

**For the dough:**
250ml (1 ¼ cups/9fl oz) whole milk
50g (3 ½ tbsp/1 ¾oz) unsalted butter
500g (3 ¾ cups/1lb 2oz) strong plain flour
75g (⅓ cup/2 ¾oz) golden caster sugar
½ tsp sea salt
1 tsp ground cinnamon
1 tsp mixed spice
¼ tsp ground nutmeg
7g (1 ½ tsp/1 sachet) fast-action dried yeast
1 egg
100ml (½ cup/3 ½fl oz) orange juice
200g (1 ½ cups/7oz) sultanas and mixed peel

1. Brush a 12-cup Bundt® pan with butter.

2. Pour the milk into a small saucepan and add the butter. Place over a low heat to warm the milk and melt the butter.

3. Add the flour, sugar, salt and spices to the bowl of a stand mixer fitted with a dough hook. Sprinkle over the yeast, then pour over the butter and milk and mix on medium speed. Add the egg and mix until smooth and elastic – this will take about 10 minutes. Place the dough into a lightly oiled bowl, cover with clingfilm and leave for 1–2 hours until doubled in size.

4. Heat the orange juice in a saucepan and add the sultanas to rehydrate them. Bring to a simmer and leave them to soak up the juice until ready to use.

5. Knock the dough back by kneading briefly and then fold the sultanas and mixed peel through it. Shape the dough into a ball. Use the end of a wooden spoon to make a hole in the centre of the ball, then pick it up by the hole to stretch it and place it in the prepared pan over the central core of the pan (so the dough is seamless). Cover with clingfilm and leave to rise for 30 minutes.

**For the crosses:**
50g (⅓ cup/1¾oz) plain flour
50ml (¼ cup/2fl oz) water
1 tbsp caster sugar
1 tbsp butter

**For the glaze:**
4 tbsp apricot jam

**To serve:**
Mini chocolate eggs

6. Preheat your oven to 180°C fan/200°C/400°F/gas 4.

7. Bake the Bundt for 25 minutes. While it is baking, whisk together the flour, water and sugar for the crosses and put this mixture into a piping bag. Remove the Bundt from the oven and invert it onto a baking tray. Pipe a circle over the top, then 4 lines from the centre to the outside to create crosses. Return to the oven for a further 5–10 minutes.

8. Heat the apricot jam and then pass it through a sieve. Brush it all over the top of the hot cross Bundt to make it shine. Fill the centre with mini chocolate eggs and serve with joy for your Easter breakfast. Breads are always best the day they're made but this will keep you going over the Easter weekend, toasted and smothered in butter.

# Cornish Saffron Bundt

I've only ever eaten pillowy, sultana-dotted Cornish saffron buns in Cornwall
(or those I've made in my own home), which makes them something of a treat
as they remind me of carefree beach days with sun, salt and sand. Historically,
crocus flowers were grown in Cornwall, so when their saffron was harvested it was
only natural that local dishes would include it, and although there aren't as many
crocuses these days, the saffron buns stand strong! Apart from the delightful yellow
tone, saffron adds a gentle mellowness of flavour that is only enhanced by a
good smothering of proper Cornish clotted cream and jam.

SERVES 8

**For the 12-cup Anniversary
    Bundt® pan:**
Butter, melted

**For the dough:**
250ml (1 ¼ cups/9fl oz)
    whole milk
A big pinch of saffron strands
60g (½ stick/1 ¼oz) unsalted
    butter
100ml (½ cup/3 ½fl oz) clotted
    cream (or double cream)
500g (3 cups/1lb 2oz) strong
    bread flour
7g (1 ½ tsp/1 sachet) fast-
    action dried yeast
75g (½ cup/2 ¾oz) caster sugar
7g (1 ½ tsp) salt
20g (¼ cup/¾oz) sultanas
20g (¼ cup/¾oz) raisins
20g (¼ cup/¾oz) mixed peel

**For the sugar glaze:**
2 tbsp caster sugar
2 tbsp boiling water

**To serve:**
Jam of your choice
Clotted cream

1. Brush a 12-cup Anniversary Bundt® pan with butter.

2. Pour the milk into a saucepan and add the saffron. Heat the milk
   to almost boiling, then remove from the heat and leave to infuse
   and turn a warm golden yellow.

3. Return the saucepan to the heat and add the butter and cream.
   Heat gently to melt everything together and then set it aside.

4. Put the flour, yeast, sugar and salt together into a mixing bowl
   – or the bowl of a stand mixer fitted with the dough hook – and
   make a well in the centre. Pour in the saffron milk and mix until
   the dough comes together. The dough will be a little scraggy but
   knead it for 10 minutes until it is smooth and elastic. Place in a
   lightly oiled bowl and cover with clingfilm. Leave in a warm place
   for about 1 hour until doubled in size.

5. Preheat your oven to 180°C fan/200°C /400°F/gas 6.

6. Remove the dough from the bowl and knock back by kneading for
   a couple of minutes then fold in the sultanas, raisins and mixed
   peel. Roll into a smooth ball. Take a wooden spoon and make
   a hole in the centre of the dough. Pick the dough up by holding
   the hole and stretching it so that it fits into the prepared pan
   over the central core (and looks neat without a seam). Bake for
   30–35 minutes or until it is golden and feels hollow when tapped
   underneath. Invert onto a wire rack to cool.

7. To make the glaze, mix the sugar and water together, then use a
   pastry brush to brush over the top of the saffron bread. Serve warm
   with jam and clotted cream. This bread is best eaten on the day
   of making but tastes delicious toasted for a couple of days after.

# Pumpkin Brioche Bundt

———

This, for me, is a Sunday bake. A quiet early morning before everyone
else is up and then the smell wafts alluringly through the house (although
I don't think anything gets teenagers out of bed).

SERVES 8

125ml (⅔ cup/4floz) whole
   milk, lukewarm
50g (¼ cup/1¾oz) caster
   sugar
1 tsp salt
7g (1½ tsp/1 sachet) fast-
   action dried yeast
500g (3 cups/1lb 2oz) plain
   flour
5 medium eggs
175g (2½ sticks/6oz) unsalted
   butter, cubed, at room
   temperature
100g (½ cup/3½oz) pumpkin
   purée
1 egg, beaten, for brushing

**For the apricot glaze:**
50g (3 tbsp/1¾oz) apricot jam
1 tbsp water

**To serve:**
Cinnamon butter

1. To the bowl of a stand mixer fitted with the dough hook, add the lukewarm milk and sugar to one side, salt to the other, and sprinkle over the yeast. Leave for around 15 minutes until frothy. (If there are no bubbles, your yeast may no longer be active, in which case you need to start again with new yeast.)

2. Add the flour to the bowl and with the stand mixer set on a low speed, mix in the yeast and add the eggs one at a time, pausing between each addition to make sure they are fully incorporated. Put the mixer on to medium and add the butter, one cube at a time. Keep mixing between each addition then finally add the pumpkin purée, also a spoonful at a time. This will take about 10 minutes, at the end of which the dough should be soft and elastic.

3. Place the dough in a lightly oiled bowl covered with clingfilm. Leave to rise in a warm place for about 2 hours until doubled in size.

4. Once doubled in size, put the dough in the refrigerator and chill for at least 2 hours (and up to 24 hours).

5. Remove the dough from the refrigerator, knead it briefly to knock it back, then portion into 8 pieces. Roll each piece into a ball and space evenly around a 12-cup Bundt® pan. Cover with clingfilm and leave to rise for a final 30 minutes.

6. Preheat your oven to 160°C fan/180°C/350°F/gas 4.

7. Brush the dough with the beaten egg, then bake in your oven, on the middle shelf, for 40–45 minutes.

8. Place the apricot jam and water in a small heatproof bowl and microwave until runny. Pass through a sieve. While the brioche Bundt is still piping hot, brush the apricot glaze all over it to make it shine. Leave to cool in the pan for 20 minutes. Serve sliced, warm, with cinnamon butter. Brioche is at its best on the day it's made but warm gently to enjoy the next day.

# Honey & Sesame Challah Bundt

I first ate challah at my friends' grandmother's house in Austria. We would sit at her breakfast table with hot milk in old-fashioned teacups and although I was only eight, I shared in her delight as she brought her freshly baked bread to the table and had no idea that those moments would stay with me forever.

SERVES 6

**For the 12-cup Bundt® pan:**
Vegetable oil, for greasing

**For the dough:**
120ml (½ cup/4fl oz) lukewarm water
75g (¼ cup/2½oz) honey
7g (1½ tsp/1 sachet) fast-action dried yeast
500g (3 cups/1lb 2oz) strong bread flour, plus extra for dusting
1 tsp salt
3 eggs
60ml (¼ cup/2fl oz) vegetable oil, plus extra for greasing
70g (½ cup/2½oz) sesame seeds
1 egg, lightly beaten

**To serve:**
Butter
Thick-set honey
Sesame seeds

1. Lightly oil a 12-cup Bundt® pan.

2. Take a jug and add the water, 1 tablespoon of the honey and the yeast. Mix briefly and set aside for 15 minutes so the yeast is activated and frothy.

3. To the bowl of a stand mixer fitted with the dough hook, add the flour and salt, then pour in the yeast mixture and mix until combined. Add the remaining honey, eggs and oil and mix on a medium speed for about 10 minutes until the dough is smooth and elastic. Place the dough in a lightly oiled bowl and cover with clingfilm. Place somewhere warm for 1–1½ hours until doubled in size.

4. When the dough has doubled in size, remove from the bowl and place on a lightly floured surface. Divide the dough into one-third and two-thirds. Roll the two-thirds piece into 8 balls and the smaller piece into 8 smaller balls. Roll the smaller balls in sesame seeds and then arrange the larger and smaller balls alternately in the prepared Bundt® pan. Cover with clingfilm again and leave to rise for 1 hour until doubled in size.

5. Preheat your oven to 160°C fan/180°C/350°F/gas 4.

6. Brush the risen challah with the beaten egg and bake for 30–35 minutes. Remove from the tin and cool on a wire rack.

7. Serve with butter, thick-set honey and an extra sprinkling of toasted sesame seeds. This bread is best eaten on the day it's made but can be enjoyed warmed or toasted over the next few days.

# Pull-apart Caramel & Pecan Monkey Bread

———

Monkey bread should come with a warning: it's too delicious and therefore
irresistible! It's made from small balls, like cinnamon-caramel doughnuts,
and as you pull them apart you get strings of gooey caramel.

**SERVES 8**

**For the 12-cup Anniversary Bundt® pan:**
30g (2 tbsp/1oz) unsalted butter

**For the dough:**
175ml (¾ cup + 2 tbsp/6fl oz) whole milk
75g (⅔ stick/2¾oz) unsalted butter
500g (3 cups/1lb 2oz) strong bread flour
7g (1½ tsp/1 sachet) fast-action dried yeast
50g (¼ cup/1¾oz) caster sugar
1 tsp salt
1 egg

**For coating:**
175g (1½ sticks/6oz) unsalted butter, melted
200g (1 cup/7oz) dark muscovado sugar
2 tsp ground cinnamon
75g (¾ cup/2¾oz) pecans, lightly toasted and chopped

**For the drizzle:**
200g (1⅓ cups/7oz) icing sugar
4 tbsp whole milk

1. Generously grease a 12-cup Anniversary Bundt® pan.

2. Gently heat the milk and butter together in a small saucepan over a low heat. The milk shouldn't ever feel hot.

3. Add the flour, yeast, sugar and salt to the bowl of a stand mixer fitted with the dough hook. Mix together to combine. Pour over the milk mixture, add the egg and mix until smooth – this will take about 10 minutes. It will be a bit sticky but scrape down the sides and bring the dough together to form one smooth ball, then cover the bowl with clingfilm. Put the bowl somewhere warm for 1–2 hours until doubled in size.

4. Place the dough on to a clean surface (there shouldn't be any need to flour it), then divide the mixture in half, then in quarters, then eighths etc, until you have 64 pieces.

5. Put the butter into a small saucepan and melt gently, then remove from the heat. Put the sugar and cinnamon into a bowl. Roll the pieces of dough into balls. Drop 12 dough balls into the melted butter and then use a fork to lift them into the sugar and cinnamon. Toss them to coat all over, then put them into the prepared pan. Repeat with all the dough balls but when you're halfway through scatter over the pecans. When putting the balls into the Bundt® pan don't worry about any spaces as they will all be filled when risen and baked. Cover the Bundt® pan with clingfilm and put somewhere warm to rise for 1 hour.

6. Preheat your oven to 160°C fan/180°C/350°F/gas 4.

7. Bake the monkey bread for 35–40 minutes. Leave to cool in the pan for at least 20 minutes and then invert onto a serving plate.

8. To make the drizzle, simply mix the icing sugar and milk together and drizzle back and forth over the monkey bread. This is best eaten on the day it's made and serving it warm is always delicious.

# Cinnamon Croissant Bundt

———

You might have to put your chef's hat on for this one as it is a little more demanding. The real question is: is it worth the effort? I can't even begin to explain how well worth it every flaky, buttery, cinnamon-sugared layer actually is. The dough is made from a combination of a croissant dough mixed with a yeasted doughnut dough, which come together to make a totally delicious Bundt. Yum!

SERVES 6

**For the dough:**
500g (3 cups/1lb 2oz) strong bread flour
50g (¼ cup/1¾oz) caster sugar
3 tsp salt
7g (1½ tsp/1 sachet) fast-action dried yeast
100ml (½ cup/3½fl oz) whole milk
5 eggs
25g (2 tbsp/1oz) unsalted butter, softened
Vegetable oil, for greasing
Plain flour, for dusting (optional)
250g (2 sticks + 3 tbsp/9oz) unsalted butter, divided into 3 pieces, chilled
1 egg, beaten

**For the filling:**
125g (½ cup/4½oz) light muscovado sugar
4 tbsp ground cinnamon

**For the glaze:**
50g (3 tbsp/1¾oz) apricot jam
1 tbsp water

1. Add the flour, sugar, salt, yeast and milk to the bowl of a stand mixer fitted with the dough hook. Mix together on a medium speed, then add the eggs, one at a time. Once they're fully incorporated, add the softened butter and mix for 10–15 minutes or until the dough is smooth and elastic. Scrape the dough out into a lightly oiled bowl, cover in clingfilm and leave in a warm place for 1½–2 hours until risen.

2. Knock back the dough and knead very briefly to shape into a ball, then return to the bowl, cover with clingfilm and refrigerate for at least 2 hours (and up to 24 hours).

3. Remove the dough from the refrigerator and tip on to a clean surface. It's a good idea to have some plain flour to hand in case it sticks. Roll the dough out into a rectangle roughly 20 x 45cm (8 x 17¾in). Use a palette knife to gently press from all sides to create a rectangle with square corners, with a short end facing you. Take your first one-third of the chilled butter. Cut it into small cubes or slices and arrange them over two-thirds of the dough, leaving the top third empty. Fold the top third of dough down and the bottom third up (like a letter), so you're left with a rectangle roughly the same size as you started with. This is to create the buttery layers. If the butter seeps through at all, add a little flour and brush any excess off with a pastry brush. Now, turn the dough so the open edge is facing you and repeat the whole process of rolling it out into a rectangle and folding but this time without adding any butter. Wrap in clingfilm and refrigerate for 30 minutes. Then repeat the same roll and fold process again with the second third of the butter.

Method continued overleaf →

4. Bring the dough out for a final roll and fold with the last third of butter. Cover in clingfilm again and refrigerate until ready to bake or use immediately. At this stage you can also freeze it for 2 months and defrost completely before using.

5. Roll out the dough into a large rectangle with the long end facing you, roughly 40 x 55cm (16 x 22in). Mix the sugar and cinnamon together and sprinkle the dough with the cinnamon sugar. Roll up the dough from a long end so you have a Swiss roll. Cut it into 8 even pieces, then place them on an angle in the base of a 12-cup Anniversary Bundt® pan. Cover with clingfilm and leave somewhere warm to rise for 30 minutes, or until doubled in size.

6. Preheat your oven to 160°C fan/180°C/350°F/gas 4.

7. Brush the dough sparingly with the beaten egg and bake for 30–35 minutes.

8. Leave to cool in the pan for 10 minutes and then transfer to a serving plate. It will look pretty either way up!

9. Warm the apricot jam and water either in a small saucepan or a microwave and brush generously over the croissant bundt.Serve warm for an indulgent weekend breakfast or simply just because. This is enjoyed best on the day it's made, especially when warm and fresh from the oven. Gently warm to enjoy the day after.

# Babka Bundt

---

Babka sits somewhere in between bread and cake. Irresistible any time of day it is so versatile, as a whole range of flavours can be added to it (see pages 184–187 for suggestions).

**SERVES 8**

**For the 12-cup Bundt® pan:**
Cake release spray (see page 240 for homemade)

**For the babka:**
1 tsp vanilla extract
120ml (⅔ cup/4fl oz) whole milk, lukewarm
7g (1½ tsp/1 sachet) fast-action dried yeast
500g (3 cups/1lb 2oz) plain flour
3 eggs
75g (⅓ cup/2¾oz) caster sugar
A pinch of salt
85g (¾ stick/3oz) unsalted butter, cubed, at room temperature
Vegetable oil, for greasing
Filling of your choice (see pages 184–187)
1 egg, beaten

**For the apricot glaze:**
50g (3 tbsp/1¾oz) apricot jam
1 tbsp water

1. Prepare a 12-cup Bundt® pan by spraying with cake release spray or brushing with homemade version.

2. To the bowl of a stand mixer fitted with the dough hook, add the vanilla extract and lukewarm milk and then sprinkle over the yeast. Leave for around 15 minutes until frothy. (If there are no bubbles, your yeast may no longer be active, in which case you need to start again with new yeast.)

3. With the stand mixer set on low speed, add the flour in a few batches. Once it's been fully incorporated, add the eggs, one at a time, pausing between each addition to make sure they are fully incorporated. Add the caster sugar, then the salt, again mixing well. Finally, take the butter and add it one cube at a time. Mix between each addition. Put the mixer on to a higher speed and mix until smooth.

4. Remove the dough from the stand mixer and knead by stretching and pulling to ensure it's ready to rest. It should stretch to your shoulder if the gluten has developed. Shape the dough into a ball and place in a lightly oiled bowl covered with clingfilm. Leave to rise in a warm place for about 1 hour until doubled in size.

5. Take the dough and roll it out on a large piece of clingfilm (or silicone mat) into a rectangle around 30 x 40cm (12 x 16in). Cover with second layer of clingfilm and refrigerate for at least 1 hour (or up to 24 hours).

6. Remove the dough from the refrigerator. Roll it out a little further and then choose a filling from pages 184–187 and spread it over the dough. Starting from a long side, roll up the dough. Cut in half so you have 2 long Swiss rolls, then twist them around each other, join the ends and place in the prepared pan. Cover with clingfilm and leave to rise for about 30 minutes.

7. Preheat your oven to 180°C fan/200°C/400°F/gas 6.

8. Brush the dough with the beaten egg, then bake in the oven, on the middle shelf, for 20–25 minutes.

9. Place the apricot jam and water in a small heatproof bowl and microwave until runny. Pass through a sieve. While the babka is still piping hot, brush the apricot glaze all over it to make it shine. Leave to cool in the pan for 15 minutes and then remove to a wire rack. Serve sliced, warm. This is best enjoyed the day it's made but could be warmed in a low oven the following day.

# Chocolate Hazelnut Babka

———————

I like that babka isn't sweet like cake but also not simply bread, it sits somewhere in between, which I think makes it perfect for a weekend brunch. With its Nutella swirls and squishy bread that pulls apart in delicious pieces it's hard to resist and apparently tastes especially good dipped into a hot chocolate (or so Lilybee tells me).

SERVES 8

**For the 12-cup Bundt® pan:**
Butter, melted

**For the babka:**
50g (¼ cup/1¾oz) hazelnuts
Babka Bundt dough (page 182)
200g (1 cup/7oz) chocolate
　　hazelnut spread (I use
　　Nutella)
1 egg, beaten

**For the apricot glaze:**
50g (3 tbsp/1¾oz) apricot jam
1 tbsp water

1. Preheat your oven to 160°C fan/180°C/350°F/gas 4. Brush a 12-cup Bundt® pan with melted butter and set aside until ready to use.

2. Put the whole hazelnuts on a baking sheet and gently roast them for about 5 minutes. Remove from the oven and increase the temperature to 180°C fan/200°C/400°F/gas 6. After the hazelnuts have cooled, chop them.

3. When the babka dough is stretched out (see page 182), spread the chocolate hazelnut spread over it and scatter with the roast hazelnuts. Starting from a long side, roll up the dough. Cut in half so you have 2 long Swiss rolls, then twist them around each other, join the ends and place in the prepared pan. Cover with clingfilm and leave to rise for about 30 minutes.

4. Brush the dough with the beaten egg and then bake in the oven, on the middle shelf, for 20–25 minutes.

5. Place the apricot jam and water in a small heatproof bowl and microwave until runny. Pass through a sieve. While the babka is still piping hot, brush the apricot glaze all over it to make it shine. Leave to cool in the pan for 15 minutes, then remove to a wire rack. Serve sliced, warm. A babka is best eaten the day it's made but could also be enjoyed the following day when warmed in a low oven.

# Tahini & Chocolate Babka

I suppose tahini and chocolate are the elegant version of a peanut butter
cup, and as a combination it does have a very similar kind of charm.

SERVES 8

**For the 10-cup Bundt® pan:**
Butter, melted

**For the babka:**
75g (⅓ cup/2¾oz) tahini
75g (⅓ cup/2¾oz) caster
   sugar
75g (⅔ stick/2¾oz) unsalted
   butter
75g (5 tbsp/2¾oz) dark
   chocolate
Babka Bundt dough (page 182)
1 egg, beaten
3 tbsp sesame seeds

**For the apricot glaze:**
50g (3 tbsp/1¾oz) apricot jam
1 tbsp water

1. Brush a 10-cup Bundt® pan with melted butter and set aside
   until ready to use.

2. To prepare the tahini filling, gently melt the tahini, sugar, butter
   and chocolate together in a small saucepan. Transfer to a cold
   bowl to thicken.

3. When the babka dough is stretched out (see page 182), spread
   the tahini mixture over the dough. Starting from a long side, roll
   up the dough. Cut in half so you have 2 long Swiss rolls, then
   twist them around each other, join the ends and place in the
   prepared pan. Cover with clingfilm and leave to rise for about
   30 minutes.

4. Preheat your oven to 180°C fan/200°C/400°F/gas 6.

5. Brush the dough with the beaten egg and then bake in the oven,
   on the middle shelf, for 20–25 minutes.

6. Place the apricot jam and water in a small heatproof bowl and
   microwave until runny. Pass through a sieve. While the babka
   is still piping hot, brush the apricot glaze all over it to make it
   shine. Scatter over the sesame seeds. Leave to cool in the pan
   for 15 minutes, then remove to a wire rack. Serve sliced, warm.
   Babkas are always best on the day they're made (and still warm!)
   but they retain their charm when warmed in a low oven the
   following day too.

# Apple & Cinnamon Babka

Apple and cinnamon give a far more subtle colouring to the babka but
I think this gentleness is really delightful. Caramelised apples and
cinnamon are, for me, the perfect breakfast babka.

SERVES 8

**For the 10-cup Bundt® pan:**
Butter, melted

**For the babka:**
60g (½ stick/2¼oz) unsalted
 butter
100g (½ cup/3½oz) light
 muscovado sugar
6 apples, peeled and cut into
 small dice
2 tsp ground cinnamon
Babka Bundt dough (page 182)
1 egg, beaten
100g (½ cup/3½oz) flaked
 almonds, toasted

**For the apricot glaze:**
50g (3 tbsp/1¾oz) apricot jam
1 tbsp water

1. Brush a 10-cup Bundt® pan with melted butter and set aside until ready to use.

2. Melt the butter in a frying pan and add the sugar. Heat until you have a syrupy consistency and then add the diced apple and cinnamon and toss to coat in the caramelised sugar. Cook for around 5 minutes until the apple is almost soft. Tip the filling into a cold bowl, cover with clingfilm and chill in your refrigerator until ready to fill your babka.

3. When the babka dough is stretched out (see page 182), spread the apple mixture over the dough. Starting from a long side, roll up the dough. Cut in half so you have 2 long Swiss rolls, then twist them around each other, join the ends and place in the prepared pan. Cover with clingfilm and leave to rise for about 30 minutes.

4. Preheat your oven to 180°C fan/200°C/400°F/gas 6.

5. Brush the dough with the beaten egg and then bake in the oven, on the middle shelf, for 20–25 minutes.

6. Place the apricot jam and water in a small heatproof bowl and microwave until runny. Pass through a sieve. While the babka is still piping hot, brush the apricot glaze all over it to make it shine. Scatter over the toasted flaked almonds. Leave to cool in the pan for 15 minutes, then remove to a wire rack. Serve sliced, warm. Babka is always at its best on the day it's made but it will still taste delicious the following day when warmed in a low oven.

# Chocolate Peanut Babka

This is a fun babka to make you smile and the chocolate-coated peanuts really do add something to the whole enjoyment.

SERVES 8

**For the 12-cup Bundt® pan:**
Butter, melted

**For the babka:**
75g (⅓ cup/2¾oz) caster sugar
75g (⅔ stick/2¾oz) unsalted butter
75g (5 tbsp/2¾oz) dark chocolate
Babka Bundt dough (page 182)
140g (1 cup/5oz) chocolate-coated peanuts (I use peanut M&Ms)
1 egg, beaten

**For the apricot glaze:**
50g (3 tbsp/1¾oz) apricot jam
1 tbsp water

1. Brush melted butter in a 12-cup Anniversary Bundt® pan and set aside until ready to use.

2. Melt the caster sugar and butter together in a small saucepan over a gentle heat. Remove from the heat and add the chocolate, then let it sit to melt. Pour into a cold bowl and refrigerate until ready to use.

3. When the babka dough is ready and stretched out (see page 182), use a spatula to spread the chocolate mixture all over it, then scatter the chocolate-coated peanuts over the top. Starting from a long side, roll up the dough. Cut in half so you have 2 long Swiss rolls, then twist them around each other, join the ends and place in the prepared pan. Cover with clingfilm and leave to rise for about 30 minutes.

4. Preheat your oven to 180°C fan/200°C/400°F/gas 6.

5. Brush the dough with the beaten egg and then bake in the oven, on the middle shelf, for 20–25 minutes.

6. Place the apricot jam and water in a small heatproof bowl and microwave until runny. Pass through a sieve. While the babka is still piping hot, brush the apricot glaze all over it to make it shine. Leave to cool in the pan for 15 minutes, then remove to a wire rack. Serve sliced, warm. Babkas taste best on the day they're made but will keep until the following day. Heating in a low oven to warm gives great results.

Image overleaf →

# Bundtnuts

A single baked doughnut recipe that is then dressed in so many ways to create a different experience each time (see pages 191–196 for ideas for glazes). So I had to ensure it was a doughnut that dreams are made of with the right amount of squishiness and overall YUM!

MAKES 12

**For the Bundtlette® pans:**
25g (2 tbsp/1oz) butter, melted
25g (2 tbsp/1oz) plain flour

**For the bundnuts:**
50g (4 tbsp/1¾oz) unsalted butter, softened
100g (½ cup/3½oz) golden caster sugar
100g (½ cup/3½oz) light muscovado sugar
2 eggs
1 tsp vanilla bean paste
1 tsp ground cinnamon
½ tsp ground nutmeg
½ tsp salt
250ml (1¼ cups/9fl oz) whole milk
250g (1½ cups/9oz) self-raising flour
Glaze of your choice (see pages 191–196)

1. Preheat your oven to 180°C fan/200°C/400°F/gas 6.

2. Brush two Anniversary Bundtlette® pans with melted butter and sift over the plain flour. Tip out the excess and set aside until ready to use.

3. Add the butter and sugars to a mixing bowl. Beat until smooth, then add the eggs, vanilla, cinnamon, nutmeg and salt. Add the milk and finally pour in the flour and mix until smooth. Pour the batter into the prepared pans.

4. Bake the Bundtnuts for 15–18 minutes. Leave to cool in the pans for 10–15 minutes and then invert onto a wire rack ready for glazing. The only problem will be choosing which glaze to go for! These are best on the day they're made but can also be frozen for up to a month. This is a great method of making them as a treat and you just want to make them individually.

# Classic

---

MAKES 12

165g (1½ sticks/5¾oz)
   butter, melted
165g (¾ cup/5¾oz) caster
   sugar
Bundnuts (page 190)

Fairground appeal forever!

1. Melt the butter in a small saucepan over a gentle heat. Remove from the heat. Pour the sugar into a small shallow dish.

2. One at a time, dip each Bundtnut into the melted butter (or you could use a pastry brush to brush them instead of dipping) and then roll them in the sugar so they're covered on all sides.

3. Delicious served warm. They will keep in an airtight container for a couple of days but are best eaten on the day they're made.

---

# Classic Glazed

---

MAKES 12

100g (½ cup/4oz) butter
2 tbsp golden syrup
250g (1½ cups/9oz) icing
   sugar
Bundnuts (page 190)

My daughter loves a classic glazed doughnut, so that's what I was aiming for with this one and it's remarkably close.

1. Melt the butter and golden syrup in a small saucepan over a gentle heat. Remove from the heat. Pour into a small shallow dish and mix with half of the icing sugar.

2. One at a time, dip each Bundtnut into the melted butter (or you could use a pastry brush to brush them instead of dipping) and then roll them in the remaining icing sugar so they're covered on all sides.

3. Serve warm. They will keep in an airtight container for a couple of days.

# Sugar Spiced

MAKES 12

A classic Bundtnut for all seasons!

165g (1 ½ sticks/5¾oz) butter
165g (¾ cup/5¾oz) caster
    sugar
1 tsp ground nutmeg
3 tbsp ground cinnamon
Bundnuts (page 190)

1. Melt the butter in a small saucepan over a gentle heat. Remove from the heat. Pour the sugar, nutmeg and cinnamon into a small shallow dish and mix them together.

2. One at a time, dip each Bundtnut into the melted butter (or you could use a pastry brush to brush them instead of dipping) and then roll them in the spiced sugar so they're covered on all sides.

3. Serve warm. They will keep in an airtight container for a couple of days. Any leftover spiced sugar will keep for other bakes and pancakes or waffles.

# Tahini Glaze

MAKES 12

These are Bundtnuts elevated to something you can share with the grown-ups.

4 tbsp tahini
3 tbsp maple syrup
1 tbsp whole milk
200g (1 ½ cups/7oz) icing
    sugar
Bundnuts (page 190)
1 tbsp black sesame seeds

1. Melt the tahini, maple syrup and milk in a small saucepan over a gentle heat. Pour over the icing sugar and mix until smooth.

2. One at a time, dip each Bundtnut into the glaze (or you could pour it over instead of dipping) so one side is covered. Sprinkle over the black sesame seeds.

3. Serve warm. They will keep in an airtight container for a couple of days but taste best on the day they're made.

# Salted Miso Caramel Glazed

MAKES 12

100g (½ cup/3½oz) white
    miso paste
300g (1½ cups/10½oz) dark
    muscovado sugar
200ml (¾ cup + 2 tbsp/7fl oz)
    double cream
1 tsp sea salt, plus extra for
    sprinkling
Bundnuts (page 190)

The umami flavour of a miso caramel is one that I find myself making time and time again. Where a regular caramel, as delicious as that is, has a cloying sweetness the miso takes that back a few paces, adding depth of flavour, and makes it luxurious. It also transforms a humble doughnut into something rather more grown up.

1. Melt the miso, sugar, cream and salt together in a small saucepan over a gentle heat until smooth and even. Remove from the heat. Leave to cool for around 15 minutes.

2. One at a time, dip one side of each Bundtnut into the miso caramel. Sprinkle a little salt on each one.

3. Serve warm. They will keep in an airtight container for a couple of days but are best eaten on the day they're made.

# Chocolate Sprinkles

MAKES 12

250g (1½ cups + 3 tbsp/9oz)
    icing sugar
50g (½ cup/1¾oz) cocoa
    powder
8 tbsp whole milk
1 tsp vanilla bean paste
Bundnuts (page 190)
4 tbsp chocolate sprinkles

I think these look like party Bundtnuts. They're an after-school treat to delight children, or why not send a box into school for the whole class to enjoy?

1. Whisk the icing sugar, cocoa powder, milk and vanilla together. If the mixture feels too thick, add a little more milk.

2. One at a time, dip each Bundtnut into the chocolate glaze and then scatter over chocolate sprinkles.

3. These Bundtnuts will keep in an airtight container for a couple of days but are best enjoyed on the day they're made.

# Passion Fruit Glaze

A simple zingy passion fruit turns the Bundtnut into something
more elegant.

MAKES 12

200g (2 cups/7oz) icing
    sugar, sifted
Pulp of 2 passion fruit
1 tbsp water
Bundnuts (page 190)

1. Place the icing sugar into a bowl and pour in the passion fruit
   pulp and splash of water. Mix until combined.

2. Dip one side of the Bundtnuts into the glaze and then leave
   to set.

3. These Bundnuts will keep in an airtight container for a couple
   of days but taste best on the day they're made.

CHAPTER 9

——

# Celebration Bundts

# Zebra Bundt with Chocolate Frosting

A vanilla zebra with chocolate stripes or a chocolate zebra with vanilla stripes? Either way it's a deliciously decorative surprise hidden beneath a chocolate fudge frosting that makes it a great choice for a children's celebration.

SERVES 12

**For the 12-cup Anniversary Bundt® Pan:**
15g (1 tbsp/½oz) butter
15g (1 tbsp/½oz) plain flour

**For the cake:**
50g (⅓ cup/1¾oz) cocoa powder
75ml (⅓ cup/2½fl oz) boiling water
325g (3 sticks/11½oz) unsalted butter, melted
500g (2¼ cups/1lb 2oz) caster sugar
5 eggs
1 tsp vanilla bean paste
360g (3 cups/12½oz) plain flour
2 tsp baking powder

1. Preheat your oven to 160°C fan/180°C/350°F/gas 4.

2. Melt the butter, then use a pastry brush to brush it generously over the inside of a 12-cup Anniversary Bundt® pan, being careful to get into every nook and cranny. I find it easier to brush from the base up to prevent any butter pooling. Sift over the flour, moving the pan from side to side to coat it evenly, then tap it while inverted to remove any excess flour. Set aside until ready to use.

3. In a small bowl, whisk together the cocoa powder and boiling water until you have a paste, mixing well so the colour is even. Set aside to cool while you prepare the cake batter.

4. Using hand-held electric beaters, combine the melted butter and sugar in a large bowl. Break in the eggs, pour in the vanilla and continue to beat until fully incorporated. Add the flour and baking powder and beat until just combined.

5. Place half the mixture in a separate bowl and add the prepared cocoa paste. Spoon a ladle of the vanilla mixture into the prepared Bundt® pan. Using the same-sized spoon, spoon a chocolate spoonful on top so that it doesn't go beyond the outer line of the vanilla spoonful. Give the Bundt® pan a little jiggle to make the batters spread out and then wait a few minutes for them to settle. Add the next spoonful and repeat until you've used all the batter. Creating these layers will take about 15 minutes, but those zebra stripes will be worth it!

**For the chocolate frosting:**

50g (¼ cup/1¾oz) dark
  chocolate, 70% cocoa solids
110g (1 stick/3¾oz) unsalted
  butter, softened
250g (1 ⅔ cup/9oz) icing
  sugar, sifted
40g (¼ cup/1¼oz) cocoa
  powder, sifted
A pinch of salt
60ml (¼ cup/2fl oz) soured
  cream
35ml (4 tbsp/1fl oz) boiling
  water
1 tsp vanilla bean paste

**To decorate (optional):**

Fancy-dressed zebras
Sprinkles

6. Bake for 1 hour–1 hour 5 minutes or until a skewer inserted into the cake comes out clean. Leave to cool in the pan for 30 minutes and then invert onto a serving plate to cool completely.

7. To make the frosting, place the chocolate in a heatproof bowl and microwave until melted. Stir with a fork until smooth. Place all the remaining frosting ingredients in a mixing bowl, add the melted chocolate and beat them together. Mix until smooth and refrigerate until ready to frost your cake.

8. Once the Bundt has cooled, use a palette knife to spread the chocolate frosting over it and leave to set. Decorate with fancy-dressed zebras or simply add sprinkles and enjoy! This cake is best eaten on the day it's made but will keep fully made if refrigerated a day ahead. Bring to room temperature before serving.

Image on page 204

# Tiger Bundt with Chocolate Frosting

I love the surprise element of both the zebra (see page 200) and tiger cakes. A seemingly innocent chocolate Bundt has the big reveal moment of cutting into it and seeing those whimsical stripes. Is it vanilla cake with chocolate stripes or chocolate cake with vanilla ones? The stripes aren't difficult to create but do take a little patience.

SERVES 10

**For the 12-cup Anniversary Bundt® pan:**
15g (1 tbsp/½oz) butter
15g (1 tbsp/½oz) plain flour

**For the cake:**
50g (⅓ cup/1¾oz) cocoa powder
75ml (⅓ cup/2½fl oz) boiling water
325g (3 sticks/11½oz) unsalted butter, melted
500g (2¼ cups/1lb 2oz) caster sugar
5 eggs
1 tsp vanilla bean paste
360g (3 cups/12½oz) plain flour
2 tsp baking powder
2 tsp orange food colouring

1. Preheat your oven to 160°C fan/180°C/350°F/gas 4.

2. Melt the butter, then use a pastry brush to brush it generously over the inside of a 12-cup Anniversary Bundt® pan, being careful to get into every nook and cranny. I find it easier to brush from the base up to prevent any butter pooling. Sift over the flour, moving the pan from side to side to coat it evenly, then tap it while inverted to remove any excess flour. Set aside until ready to use.

3. In a small bowl, whisk together the cocoa powder and boiling water until you have a paste, mixing well so the colour is even. Set aside to cool while you prepare the cake batter.

4. Using hand-held electric beaters, combine the melted butter and sugar in a large bowl. Break in the eggs and pour in the vanilla bean paste and continue to beat until fully incorporated. Add the flour and baking powder and beat until just combined.

5. Place half the mixture in a separate bowl and add the prepared cocoa paste. Add the orange food colouring to the plain vanilla mixture. Spoon a ladle of the orange-vanilla mixture into the Bundt® pan. Using a same-sized spoon, spoon a chocolate spoonful on top so that it doesn't go beyond the outer line of the orange spoonful. Give the Bundt® pan a little jiggle to make them spread out and then wait a few minutes for them to settle. Add the next spoonful and repeat until you've used all the batter. Creating these layers will take about 15 minutes, but those tiger stripes will be worth it!

**For the chocolate frosting:**

50g (¼ cup/1¾oz) dark
chocolate, 70% cocoa solids

110g (1 stick/3¾oz) unsalted
butter, softened

250g (1⅔ cups/9oz) icing
sugar, sifted

40g (¼ cup/1¼oz) cocoa
powder, sifted

A pinch of salt

60ml (¼ cup/2fl oz) soured
cream

35ml (4 tbsp) boiling water

1 tsp vanilla bean paste

**To decorate (optional):**

Fancy-dressed tigers
Sprinkles

6. Bake for 1 hour–1 hour 5 minutes or until a skewer inserted into the cake comes out clean. Leave to cool in the pan for 30 minutes, then invert onto a serving plate to cool completely.

7. To make the frosting, place the chocolate in a heatproof bowl and microwave until melted. Stir with a fork until smooth. Place all the remaining frosting ingredients in a mixing bowl, add the melted chocolate and beat them together. Mix until smooth and refrigerate until ready to frost your cake.

8. Once the Bundt has cooled, use a palette knife to spread the chocolate frosting over it. Decorate with fancy-dressed tigers or simply add sprinkles and enjoy! This Bundt could be fully made and refrigerated the day before but bring to room temperature before serving. It will keep for a few days after it's made, either refrigerated or in a cool room in an airtight container.

# Rainbow Surprise with Vanilla Cream Cheese Frosting

It was while perfecting the technique for the zebra-striped cake (page 200) that I realised a similar technique could create the rainbows for this Bundt. This bake has a place in my kitchen even when no children are around because sometimes we all need a rainbow.

SERVES 8

**For the 10-cup Bavaria Bundt® pan:**
15g (1 tbsp/½oz) butter
15g (1 tbsp/½oz) plain flour

**For the cake:**
325g (3 sticks/11½oz) unsalted butter, melted
500g (2¼ cups/1lb 2oz) caster sugar
5 eggs
1 tsp vanilla bean paste
360g (3 cups/12½oz) plain flour
2 tsp baking powder
4–8 different food colourings

1. Preheat your oven to 160°C fan/180°C/350°F/gas 4.

2. Melt the butter, then use a pastry brush to brush it generously over the inside of a 10-cup Bavaria Bundt® pan, being careful to get into every nook and cranny. I find it easier to brush from the base up to prevent any butter pooling. Sift over the flour, moving the pan from side to side to coat it evenly, then tap it while inverted to remove any excess flour. Set aside until ready to use.

3. Using hand-held electric beaters, combine the melted butter and sugar in a large bowl. Add the eggs and vanilla and continue to beat until fully incorporated. Add the flour and baking powder and beat until just combined. Divide the batter between as many bowls as you have colours.

4. Spoon a scoop of the first colour of the mixture into the prepared Bundt® pan. Using the same-sized spoon, spoon a different-coloured spoonful on top so that it doesn't go beyond the outer line of the first spoonful. Give the Bundt® pan a little jiggle to make the batters spread out and then add the next spoonful. Repeat until you've used all the batter. Creating these layers will take about 15 minutes, but the rainbow result will be worth it.

5. Bake for 1 hour–1 hour 5 minutes or until a skewer inserted into the cake comes out clean. Leave to cool in the pan for 30 minutes and then invert onto a serving plate to cool completely.

**For the vanilla cream cheese frosting:**
500g (3⅓ cups/ 1lb 2oz) icing sugar
300g (1¾ cups/ 10½oz) cream cheese
1 tbsp vanilla bean paste

**To decorate:**
Funfetti

6. To make the frosting, add the icing sugar, cream cheese and vanilla to a large bowl and use hand-held electric beaters to mix them together until smooth.

7. Once the Bundt has cooled completely, use a palette knife to spread the frosting over the whole Bundt. Decorate with funfetti and slice to reveal the rainbows! This Bundt will keep for a few days in an airtight container in a cool room. If warm, keep refrigerated.

---

*Rainbow variation: For a small-scale version, make the Bundt as above, half of the frosting and then cut the Bundt in half so you have two semicircles. Freeze one semicircle. Cover the remaining semicircle with the frosting, then decorate with neat rows of coloured sugar-coated chocolates (I use M&Ms) to make a rainbow. Cover the ends of the rainbow with marshmallows to make clouds.*

Image on page 204

# Caterpillar Bundt

My niece Isabella is now in her twenties but she always loved a caterpillar cake, so this one is for her. Bright and colourful, covered in a mighty array of sweeties and chocolates it's a celebration.

SERVES 10

**For the 10-cup Bundt® pan:**
15g (1 tbsp/½oz) butter
15g (1 tbsp/½oz) caster sugar

**For the cake:**
220g (2 sticks/8oz) unsalted butter, softened
220g (1 cup/8oz) caster sugar
4 eggs
1 tsp vanilla bean paste
220g (1 cup/8oz) self-raising flour
100ml (½ cup/3½fl oz) whole milk

**For the frosting:**
500g (3 cups/1lb 2oz) icing sugar
75g (⅓ cup/2¾oz) cream cheese
25g (2 tbsp/1oz) unsalted butter, softened
A few teaspoons of food colouring of your choice or even a few to make it 'rainbow'

**To decorate:**
A selection of sweets and chocolates

1. Preheat your oven to 160°C fan/180°C/350°F/gas 4.

2. Melt the butter, then use a pastry brush to brush it generously over the inside of a 10-cup Bundt® pan, being careful to get into every nook and cranny. I find it easier to brush from the base up to prevent any butter pooling. Scatter over the sugar, moving the pan from side to side to coat it evenly, then tap it while inverted to remove any excess sugar. Set aside until ready to use.

3. Place the butter and sugar into a mixing bowl and cream together with hand-held electric beaters until very pale and very fluffy. Add the eggs and vanilla and mix again. Fold through half the flour, mix, then add the milk, followed by the remaining flour, and mix again. Pour into the prepared pan and bake for 40–45 minutes or until a skewer inserted into the cake comes out clean. Leave to cool in the pan for 15 minutes and then invert onto a wire rack to cool completely.

4. To make the frosting, beat the icing sugar, cream cheese, butter and food colouring together.

5. To assemble the inchworm, cut the Bundt in half vertically so you have 2 semicircles. Keep one semicircle and cut the other in half so you have a half and two quarters. Position the semicircle in the centre of a serving plate, standing on its ends like an arch, and add the quarters at either end. Spread the frosting all over them and use it to secure them in position. Decorate with sweets and chocolates to really bring the inchworm to life and create 'eyes', 'tentacles' and lots of little 'feet'. The centre of your party table! This Bundt is best eaten the day it's made but could be fully assembled the day before. It will keep in an airtight container in a cool room for a couple of days after.

# Sprinkles Piñata Bundt

Every Bundt is actually a piñata because the centre can always be filled, which I love as it adds a whole new layer, and for this Bundt I've really gone to town with the sprinkles so it's a child's dream.

SERVES 10

**For the 10-cup Swirl Bundt® pan:**
15g (1 tbsp/½oz) butter
15g (1 tbsp/½oz) plain flour

**For the cake:**
220g (2 sticks/8oz) unsalted butter
220g (1 cup/8oz) caster sugar
1 tsp vanilla bean paste
3 eggs
150g (½ cup/5½oz) Greek yoghurt
A pinch of salt
200g (1¼ cups/7oz) self-raising flour
30g (2 tbsp/1oz) cornflour
100g (½ cup/3½oz) sprinkles

**For the buttercream:**
110g (2 sticks/3¾oz) unsalted butter
240g (2 cups/8½oz) icing sugar
2 tbsp whole milk
½ tsp vanilla bean paste

**To decorate:**
200g (1 cup/7oz) sprinkles
200g (1 cup/7oz) sugar-coated chocolates (I use M&Ms)
100ml (½ cup/3½fl oz) whipped cream
8 glacé cherries
A mini piñata cake topper (optional)

1. Preheat your oven to 160°C fan/180°C/350°F/gas 4.

2. Melt the butter, then use a pastry brush to brush it generously over the inside of a 10-cup Swirl Bundt® pan, being careful to get into every nook and cranny. I find it easier to brush from the base up to prevent any butter pooling. Sift over the flour, moving the pan from side to side to coat it evenly, then tap it while inverted to remove any excess flour. Set aside until ready to use.

3. Add the butter and sugar to a mixing bowl. Beat until smooth, then add the vanilla and eggs, beat them in and then add the Greek yoghurt. Beat until smooth and then fold in the salt, flour and cornflour, mixing until just combined. Pour over the sprinkles and briefly fold them through. Pour the batter into the prepared pan and bake for 50–55 minutes or until a skewer inserted into the cake comes out clean. Leave to cool in the pan for 15 minutes, then invert onto a wire rack to cool completely.

4. To make the buttercream, beat the butter, icing sugar, milk and vanilla together. Slice the Bundt in half horizontally and then use a palette knife to spread some buttercream over one of the layers. Sandwich the halves back together and cover the whole cake evenly with the remaining buttercream. Once it's covered, spoon the sprinkles over, pressing them lightly on until the whole Bundt is entirely covered and looking magical.

5. To decorate, pour the chocolates into the centre, pipe rosettes of whipped cream on top and add a glacé cherry to each rosette. Add mini piñata cake toppers to finish.

Image on page 204

# Chocolate & Irish Stout Cake with Soured Cream Frosting

I don't need St Patrick's Day as an excuse to make this Bundt because it's far too delicious to save for only one day a year. The Irish stout flavour is a gentle, mellow hum in the background against the chocolate, and the soured cream frosting offers a refreshing tang.

SERVES 8

**For the 10-cup Jubilee Bundt® pan:**
15g (1 tbsp/½oz) butter
15g (1 tbsp/½oz) cocoa powder

**For the chocolate cake:**
75g (¾ cup/2¾oz) cocoa powder
300g (1½ cups/10½oz) golden caster sugar
60g (½ stick/2¼oz) unsalted butter
1 tsp vanilla bean paste
120ml (½ cup/4fl oz) boiling water
100ml (½ cup/3½fl oz) Irish stout (I use Guinness)
2 eggs, lightly beaten
175ml (¾ cup/6fl oz) soured cream
A pinch of salt
200g (1¼ cups/7oz) plain flour
1 tsp baking powder
1 tsp bicarbonate of soda

**For the soured cream frosting:**
50g (3½ tbsp/1¾oz) unsalted butter
65ml (4 tbsp/2¼fl oz) soured cream
150g (1½ cups/5½oz) icing sugar

**To decorate:**
Green sugar paste

1. Preheat your oven to 160°C fan/180°C/350°F/gas 4.

2. Melt the butter, then use a pastry brush to brush it generously over the inside of a 10-cup Jubilee Bundt® pan, being careful to get into every nook and cranny. I find it easier to brush from the base up to prevent any butter pooling. Scatter over the cocoa powder, moving the pan from side to side to coat it evenly, then tap it while inverted to remove any excess cocoa. Set aside until ready to use.

3. Add the cocoa powder, sugar, butter, vanilla and boiling water to a large mixing bowl and whisk until smooth and the butter has melted and the sugar dissolved. Pour in the stout, beaten eggs and soured cream and whisk until smooth. Fold the salt, flour, baking powder and bicarbonate of soda through, then pour into the prepared pan. Bake for 40–45 minutes or until a skewer inserted into the cake comes out clean. Leave to cool in the pan for 10 minutes on a wire rack, then invert onto the wire rack to cool completely.

4. To make the frosting, beat the butter, soured cream and icing sugar together until smooth, then spread over the top of the cooled Bundt. Decorate with green sugar paste shamrocks for St Patrick's Day! This Bundt will keep for a few days in an airtight container.

# Vanilla Cloud Cake with Bubblegum Frosting

---

This is a sensible, light and breezy cloud cake, made light by the addition of whipped egg whites, but then it's somewhat enlivened by adding bubblegum frosting, which is surprisingly delicious and perfect for a celebration.

SERVES 10

**For the 10-cup Bundt® pan:**
15g (1 tbsp/½oz) butter
15g (1 tbsp/½oz) caster sugar

**For the cake:**
220g (2 sticks/8oz) unsalted
    butter, softened
220g (1 cup/8oz) caster sugar
4 eggs, separated
1 tsp vanilla bean paste
220g (1 cup/8oz) self-raising
    flour
100ml (½ cup/3½fl oz)
    whole milk

**For the frosting:**
100g (½ cup/3½oz) cream
    cheese
400g (2¾ cups/14oz) icing sugar
1 tsp bubblegum syrup
1 tbsp milk (optional, to loosen)
Pink and blue food colouring

**To decorate:**
1 tbsp sprinkles
A mini balloon cake topper
    (optional)
Bubblegum balls (optional)

1. Preheat your oven to 140°C fan/160°C/325°F/gas 3.

2. Melt the butter, then use a pastry brush to brush it generously over the inside of a 10-cup Bundt® pan, being careful to get into every nook and cranny. I find it easier to brush from the base up to prevent any butter pooling. Sift over the sugar (this will give a delightfully sweet crust), moving the pan from side to side to coat it evenly, then tap it while inverted to remove any excess. Set aside until ready to use.

3. Place the butter and sugar (reserving 3 tablespoons in a mixing bowl. Cream with hand-held electric beaters until very pale and very fluffy. Add the egg yolks and vanilla and mix again.

4. In a separate bowl, whisk the egg whites. Beat them until doubled in size and then sprinkle in the reserved spoonfuls of sugar. Keep whisking until you can hold the bowl upside down and the egg whites stay in place. Gently fold half the flour through the egg whites so you don't deflate the air you've just put in. Add the remaining flour to the batter and mix until just combined, then fold in the egg white mixture until fully combined. Spoon into the prepared pan and bake for 40–45 minutes. Leave to cool in the pan for 20 minutes, then invert onto a wire rack to cool completely.

5. To make the frosting, beat the cream cheese and icing sugar together. Add the bubblegum syrup to taste. Divide the icing between 2 bowls and add pink food colouring to one and blue to the other. Stand the Bundt on a wire rack with a plate beneath it and pour the icing over the top. Re-use the icing caught on the plate to cover the entire Bundt. Add a few sprinkles and it's ready or decorate with a mini balloon cake topper, then fill the centre with old-fashioned bubblegum balls, if you like. It is best enjoyed the day it's made so keep in an airtight container in a cool room or refrigerate if made the day before and to keep for a few days after baking.

# Chocolate & Red Velvet Heart Bundt with Pink Mirror Glaze

This Valentine's Bundt has so many layers of love. From the heart-shaped pan to the red icing and then a surprise heart inside for someone you love!

SERVES 10

**For the red hearts:**
125g (¾ cup/4½oz) self-raising flour
125g (½ cup/4½oz) golden caster sugar
A pinch of salt
125g (1 stick + 1 tbsp/4½oz) unsalted butter, melted
2 eggs
1 tsp vanilla bean paste
Red food colouring

**For the 10-cup Elegant Heart Bundt® pan:**
15g (1 tbsp/½oz) butter
15g (1 tbsp/½oz) cocoa powder

1. Preheat your oven to 160°C fan/180°C/350°F/gas 4 and line a baking tray with a piece of baking parchment.

2. To make the hearts, take a large mixing bowl and add the flour, sugar and salt. Pour over the melted butter, eggs and vanilla and mix until smooth. Add red food colouring until you have a bright red batter. Pour it into the baking tray and bake for 25–30 minutes or until a skewer inserted into the centre comes out clean. Leave to cool completely; if it isn't completely cool the heart shapes won't be as defined. Once cool, use a heart-shaped cookie cutter (it needs to be relatively small so that it will fit within the width of the Bundt® pan) and cut hearts from the red sponge. Put the hearts in the freezer while you make the batter for the Bundt.

3. To prepare the Bundt® pan, melt the butter, then use a pastry brush to brush it generously over the inside of a 10-cup Elegant Heart Bundt® pan, being careful to get into every nook and cranny. I find it easier to brush from the base up to prevent any butter pooling. Scatter over the cocoa powder, moving the pan from side to side to coat it evenly, then tap it while inverted to remove any excess cocoa. Set aside until ready to use.

4. In a small bowl, whisk together the cocoa powder and boiling water until you have a paste. Set aside to cool while you prepare the cake batter.

5. Cream together the butter and sugar in a large bowl. Add the eggs, vanilla and buttermilk and continue to beat until fully incorporated. Add the cocoa powder paste, and mix through. Pour over the flour, baking powder, bicarbonate of soda and salt and beat until just combined. Pour half the mixture into the prepared pan.

Method and ingredients continued overleaf →

## For the bundt:
50g (½ cup/1¾oz) cocoa powder
75ml (⅓ cup/2½fl oz) boiling water
300g (2½ sticks/10½oz) unsalted butter
200g (1 cup/7oz) caster sugar
4 eggs
1 tsp vanilla bean paste
75ml (⅓ cup/2½fl oz) buttermilk
200g (1¼ cups/7oz) self-raising flour
½ tsp baking powder
½ tsp bicarbonate of soda
A pinch of salt

## For the white chocolate ganache:
225g (1¼ cups/8oz) white chocolate
225ml (1 cup/8fl oz) double cream

## For the pink mirror glaze:
230g (1⅓ cups/8oz) white chocolate
4 gelatine leaves
100ml (1 cup/3½fl oz) water
200g (1 cup + 2 tbsp/7oz) caster sugar
150g (¾ cup/5½oz) sweetened condensed milk
2 tsp red food colouring

Take the red hearts out of the freezer and arrange them upside down in a row all around the Bundt ring, with as few spaces in between them as possible. Pour the remaining batter over the hearts, then bake for 50–55 minutes or until a skewer inserted into the cake comes out clean. Leave to cool in the pan for 15 minutes, then invert onto a wire rack to cool completely.

6. To make the ganache, break the chocolate up into squares (or use chips) and place in a heatproof bowl. Heat the cream until almost boiling – I find it easiest in a microwave but you can also heat in saucepan – and then pour over the chocolate. Let it sit for 10 minutes, then stir until smooth. Place the Bundt on a wire rack with a large plate underneath and pour the ganache over the whole Bundt. Re-use the ganache caught on the plate below a few times until the Bundt is entirely covered. This layer of ganache is really important to make sure your mirror glaze is smooth. Once covered with ganache, freeze for 1 hour, so the mirror glaze will set when it touches the cold Bundt.

7. To make the mirror glaze, add the gelatine to a bowl of cold water and set aside to soften. Break up the chocolate and place in a heatproof bowl. Heat the water, sugar and condensed milk in a saucepan, bring to a simmer, then pour over the chocolate to melt it. Mix until smooth, then add the gelatine and food colouring, mixing them in, and then use a stick blender to process until velvety smooth. I find by this point the glaze is about the right temperature to pour straight over the Bundt but it should be thick, pourable and shiny. Remove the cake from the freezer, put it on a wire rack set over a plate and pour the glaze over. It's best to do this in a single pour but if you work quickly you can use the glaze from the plate below to fill any gaps. Leave the Bundt to set (and defrost) at room temperature for 30 minutes.

8. Serve with love to your Valentine! This Bundt is best served not too long after it's made so the mirror glaze keeps its shine, but it will keep in an airtight container for a few days.

# Elderflower & Raspberry Bundt with Rice Paper Butterflies

---

Mother's Day is at such a pretty time of year. Winter has been left behind and we're all rather ready for a shift into pastel colours and daffodils. All of that is reflected in this pretty, light and floral Bundt.

SERVES 8

**For the 10-cup Chiffon Bundt® pan:**
15g (1 tbsp/½oz) butter
15g (1 tbsp/½oz) plain flour

**For the cake:**
300g (2½ sticks/1⅓ cups/10½oz) unsalted butter, softened
200g (1 cup/7oz) caster sugar
4 eggs
1 tsp vanilla bean paste
200g (1¼ cups/7oz) self-raising flour
½ tsp baking powder
½ tsp bicarbonate of soda
A pinch of salt
100g (1 cup/3½oz) fresh raspberries

**For the elderflower buttercream:**
125g (⅔ cup/4½oz) cream cheese
80g (¾ stick/3oz) unsalted butter, room temperature
600g (4 cups/1lb 5oz) icing sugar
3 tbsp elderflower cordial
1 tsp pink food colouring (optional)

**To decorate:**
200g (2 cups/7oz) fresh raspberries
8 rice paper butterflies

1. Preheat your oven to 160°C fan/180°C/350°F/gas 4.

2. Melt the butter, then use a pastry brush to brush it generously over the inside of a 10-cup Chiffon Bundt® pan, being careful to get into every nook and cranny. I find it easier to brush from the base up to prevent any butter pooling. Sift over the flour, moving the pan from side to side to coat it evenly, then tap it while inverted to remove any excess flour. Set aside until ready to use.

3. Place the butter and sugar in a medium bowl and cream together until pale and fluffy. Break the eggs into a small bowl and whisk them together with the vanilla. Pour them gradually into the creamed butter and sugar and mix until fully combined. Sift over the flour, baking powder and bicarbonate of soda and fold in until just combined. Pour the batter into the prepared pan and bake for 30 minutes or until a skewer inserted into the cake comes out clean. Leave to cool in the pan for 10–15 minutes, then invert onto a wire rack to cool completely.

4. To make the buttercream, add the cream cheese, butter, icing sugar, elderflower cordial and food colouring (if using) to a mixing bowl and beat until smooth. Use a palette knife to spread over the cake or use a piping bag fitted with a plain nozzle to pipe balls of icing in a vertical line from the base and above, then use a palette knife to half squash them sideways, then pipe another row of balls and repeat.

5. To decorate, you could fill the centre with raspberries, dot a few rice paper butterflies around and serve on Mother's Day with love! This bundt will need to be refrigerated because of the buttercream but will keep for several days.

# Bee Sting Bundt with Marzipan Bees

This is an unusual cake because it's yeasted. It's essentially a brioche dough that's filled with custard and topped with sweet almonds but it's the marzipan bees that make everyone smile.

SERVES 12

**For the 10-cup Elegant Party Bundt® pan:**
Butter, for greasing

**For the cake:**
250g (1½ cups/9oz) strong bread flour
50g (¼ cup/1¾oz) caster sugar
1 tsp salt
7g (1½ tsp/1 sachet) fast-action dried yeast
50ml (¼ cup/2fl oz) whole milk
2 eggs
60g (½ stick/2¼oz) unsalted butter, softened
Neutral oil, such as vegetable, for greasing

**For the filling:**
300ml (1½ cups/10½oz) whole milk
4 egg yolks
75g (⅓ cup/2¾oz) caster sugar
15g (1 tbsp/½oz) cornflour
15g (1 tbsp/½oz) plain flour
1 tsp vanilla bean paste
150ml (⅔ cup/5fl oz) double cream

1. Butter a 10-cup Elegant Party Bundt® pan.

2. Add the flour, sugar, salt, yeast and milk to the bowl of a stand mixer fitted with the dough hook. Mix everything together on a medium speed, then add the eggs, one at a time. Once they're fully incorporated, add the butter a tablespoon at time, waiting for each to be incorporated before adding the next. Knead the dough in the stand mixer for 10–15 minutes or until the dough is smooth and elastic. It will still be a little sticky, so scrape the dough out into a lightly oiled bowl, toss it in the oil so it's coated (and therefore won't stick to the sides as it expands), then cover the bowl with clingfilm and leave in a warm place to rise for 1 hour until doubled in size.

3. Knock back the dough and knead very briefly to shape into a ball. Use the handle from a wooden spoon to make a hole in the centre, then lift it up and turn in your hands to make the hole larger and fit over the central cone of the Bundt® pan. (I like to do this so there isn't a seam.) Place the dough in the prepared pan. Cover with clingfilm and leave to rise for 30 minutes.

4. Preheat your oven to 160°C fan/180°C/350°F/gas 4. Bake for 40–45 minutes until golden and well risen. Invert onto a wire rack to cool.

5. To make the filling, put the milk in a saucepan and bring it to simmering, without letting it boil, then remove from the heat.

**For the honey topping:**
100g (¼ cup/3½oz) flaked
    almonds
110g (1 stick/3¾oz) unsalted
    butter
100g (½ cup/3½oz) light
    muscovado sugar
50g (3 tbsp/1¾oz) honey
75ml (⅓ cup/2½fl oz) double
    cream

**To decorate:**
50g (1¾oz) marzipan
30g (2 tbsp/1oz) dark chocolate
10g (1 tbsp/¼oz) flaked
    almonds

6. Put the egg yolks and caster sugar into a bowl. Whisk them together. Add the cornflour, flour and vanilla and whisk until smooth and then gradually add the milk. When all the milk has been added, return it to a clean saucepan. Heat over a medium heat and whisk vigorously until the custard is smooth. Place in a clean bowl and close cover with clingfilm so that it doesn't form a skin. Refrigerate until ready to use.

7. Softly whip the double cream, then fold it through the custard to create a crème diplomat. Slice the Bundt in half horizontally and cover the bottom half of the Bundt with the crème diplomat. Top with the other half and lightly press it down and tidy the edges with a palette knife.

8. To make the topping, put the flaked almonds in a frying pan and toast gently to release their flavour and give them colour. Set aside. Put the butter, sugar, honey and cream into a small saucepan and melt together. Turn up the heat and simmer for a few minutes, stirring, until you have a caramel. Take the saucepan off the heat and add the almonds to it. Gently mix them in, then pour over the whole Bundt. Leave to set.

9. To make the marzipan bees, roll small balls of marzipan. Melt the chocolate and use a fork to drag little lines across the marzipan, then add flaked almonds as wings. Put them on toothpicks and insert them into the cake and serve your bee-autiful Bee Sting Bundt! This bundt will keep for a couple of days if kept chilled in a refrigerator.

Image overleaf →

# Secret Bunny Bundt

There's a little Easter surprise within this delicious Bundt to delight
all your lucky guests!

**SERVES 8**

**For the Easter bunnies:**
125g (¾ cup/4½oz) self-
   raising flour
125g (½ cup/4½oz) golden
   caster sugar
A pinch of salt
125g (1 sticks + 1 tbsp/4½oz)
   unsalted butter, melted
2 eggs
1 tsp vanilla bean paste
Pink food colouring

**For the 10-cup Bavaria
   Bundt® pan:**
15g (1 tbsp/½oz) butter
15g (1 tbsp/½oz) plain flour

**For the bundt:**
300g (2½ sticks/10½oz)
   unsalted butter
200g (1 cup/7oz) caster sugar
4 eggs
½ tsp almond extract
75ml (½ cup/2½ fl oz)
   buttermilk
200g (1¼ cups/7oz) self-
   raising flour
½ tsp baking powder
½ tsp bicarbonate of soda
A pinch of salt

**To serve:**
Icing sugar

1. Preheat your oven to 160°C fan/180°C/350°F/gas 4 and line a
   baking tray with a piece of baking parchment.

2. To make the Easter bunnies, take a large mixing bowl and add
   the flour, sugar and salt. Pour over the melted butter, eggs and
   vanilla and mix until smooth. Add pink food colouring until you
   have quite a bright pink batter. Pour it into the baking tray and
   bake for 25 minutes or until a skewer inserted into the centre
   comes out clean. Leave to cool completely. Once cool, use a
   bunny-shaped cookie cutter (it needs to be relatively small so
   that it will fit within the width of the Bundt® pan) and cut bunnies
   from the pink sponge. Put the bunnies in the freezer while you
   make the batter for the Bundt.

3. To prepare the Bundt® pan, melt the butter, then use a pastry
   brush to brush it generously over the inside of a 10-cup Bavaria
   Bundt® pan, being careful to get into every nook and cranny. I
   find it easier to brush from the base up to prevent any butter
   pooling. Sift over the flour, moving the pan from side to side to
   coat it evenly, then tap it while inverted to remove any excess
   flour. Set aside until ready to use.

4. Cream together the butter and sugar in a large bowl. Add the
   eggs, almond extract and buttermilk and continue to beat
   until fully incorporated. Pour over the flour, baking powder,
   bicarbonate of soda and salt and beat until just combined.
   Pour half the mixture into the prepared pan. Take the pink
   bunnies out of the freezer and arrange them upside down in a
   row all around the Bundt ring, with as few spaces in between
   them as possible. Pour the remaining batter over the bunnies,
   then bake for 45–50 minutes or until a skewer inserted into the
   cake comes out clean. Leave to cool in the pan for 15 minutes,
   then invert onto a wire rack to cool completely.

5. Dust with icing sugar and serve as part of your Easter breakfast.
   This bundt will keep for a up to 5 days in airtight container.

# Carrot Cake with Caramel Cream Cheese Frosting

––––––––

This is a classic version of the all-American carrot cake, but as it's a Bundt there's ample room for Easter eggs in the centre.

SERVES 8

**For the 10-cup Bundt® pan:**
15g (1 tbsp/½oz) butter
15g (1 tbsp/½oz) plain flour

**For the cake:**
100g (¾ cup/3½oz) sultanas
100ml (½ cup/3½fl oz) orange juice
6 eggs
200g (1 cup + 2 tbsp/7oz) golden caster sugar
150ml (¾ cup + 1 tbsp/5fl oz) vegetable oil
30ml (2 tbsp/1fl oz) runny honey
1 tsp ground ginger
1 tsp ground cinnamon
250g (2 cups/9oz) self-raising flour
200g (1½ cups/7oz) carrots, grated
175g (1⅔ cups/7oz) pecans, chopped

**For the frosting:**
200g (1 cup/7oz) cream cheese
100g (¾ stick + 1 tbsp/3½oz) unsalted butter
600g (4 cups/1lb 5oz) icing sugar
100g (⅓ cup + 2 tbsp/3½oz) salted caramel

1. Preheat your oven to 160°C fan/180°C/350°F/gas 4.

2. Melt the butter, then use a pastry brush to brush it generously over the inside of a 10-cup Bundt® pan, being careful to get into every nook and cranny. I find it easier to brush from the base up to prevent any butter pooling. Sift over the flour, moving the pan from side to side to coat it evenly, then tap it while inverted to remove any excess flour. Set aside until ready to use.

3. Place the sultanas in a small saucepan and pour over the orange juice. Simmer gently for around 10 minutes to hydrate the sultanas.

4. In a medium bowl, whisk together the eggs and sugar, then add the oil and mix thoroughly. Add the honey and spices and mix again, before pouring in the sultanas and any remaining juice from the saucepan. Sift the self-raising flour into the wet ingredients and fold through until just combined. Stir in the grated carrot and chopped pecans, then pour the mixture into the prepared pan. Bake for 50–55 minutes or until a skewer inserted into the cake comes out clean and the top is lightly browned. Leave to cool in the pan for 15 minutes, then invert onto a wire rack to cool completely.

5. In a large bowl, beat the cream cheese, butter and icing sugar until smooth. Add the salted caramel but leave it as a swirl through the frosting and don't mix it in, keeping it streaky. Spread the frosting over the whole Bundt in an even layer. I decorated mine with baby carrots and toffee popcorn. This Bundt is best eaten on the day it's made but will keep for a couple of days in the refrigerator.

––––––––

**To decorate (optional):**
12 baby carrots with stalks
50g (8 cups/1¾oz) toffee popcorn

# Pumpkin & Chocolate Chip Bundt with Maple Filling

We have a Halloween party each year and as my daughter has got older the theme has been ever changing, but one constant that no one seems to grow out of is this pumpkin cake. It's surprisingly easy to make and uncanny that a heritage Bundt® pan transforms it so effortlessly into a pumpkin!

SERVES 16

**For the 12-cup Anniversary Bundt® pan:**
15g (1 tbsp/ ½oz) butter
15g (1 tbsp/ ½oz) plain flour

**For a cake (you will need to double this to make 2 cakes):**
375g (1 ½ cups/3 sticks/13oz) unsalted butter, softened
500g (2 ½ cups /1lb 2oz) caster sugar
6 eggs
2 tsp vanilla bean paste
A pinch of salt
325g (1 ½ cups/11 ½oz) pumpkin purée
1 tsp ground cinnamon
1 tsp ground ginger
1 tsp mixed spice
¼ tsp ground nutmeg
170g (1 cup/6oz) chocolate chips (white, milk, dark or a combination)
400g (3 cups/14oz) self-raising flour

1. Preheat your oven to 160°C fan/180°C/350°F/gas 4.

2. Melt the butter, then use a pastry brush to brush it generously over the inside of a 12-cup Anniversary Bundt® pan, being careful to get into every nook and cranny. I find it easier to brush from the base up to prevent any butter pooling. Sift over the flour, moving the pan from side to side to coat it evenly, then tap it while inverted to remove any excess flour. Set aside until ready to use.

3. Cream the butter and sugar together until pale and fluffy. Add the eggs, mix well, then add the vanilla, salt, pumpkin purée and spices. Mix well until even, then fold through the chocolate chips. Sift over the flour, mix again and pour into the prepared pan. Bake for 1 hour or until a skewer comes out clean. Leave to cool in the pan for 15 minutes, then invert onto a wire rack to cool completely. Repeat to make a second Bundt.

4. To make the frosting, beat the icing sugar, cream cheese and maple syrup together. If it feels stiff, add some milk, one teaspoon at a time.

5. Slice the uneven tops off the Bundts so you have a flat surface (reserve the cut-off layers). Then slice the Bundts horizontally in half again, creating 4 layers. Spread the maple frosting between the layers and sandwich them together so that the flat sides, the sides that would usually be your base, are now sandwiched together to create a pumpkin shape. Use a round cookie cutter to cut circles from the leftover layers and use them to fill the hole in the centre, right to the top. Refrigerate the pumpkin cake while you make the orange buttercream.

## For the maple frosting:

400g (2¾ cups/14oz) icing
   sugar
100g (½ cup/3½oz) cream
   cheese
3 tsp maple syrup
Milk, to loosen (optional)

## For the orange buttercream:

800g (5½ cups/1lb 12oz) icing
   sugar
330g (3 sticks/11½oz) unsalted
   butter
1 tbsp vanilla bean paste
1 tbsp orange food colouring,
   but you may need more
   depending type and brand
Milk, to loosen (optional)

## To decorate:

Green and brown sugar paste
Edible glitter

6. To make the buttercream, beat the icing sugar, butter, vanilla and food colouring together. As it's such a large quantity it's best to do this with either hand-held electric beaters or in a stand mixer. Add the food colouring little by little until you have your desired shade of orange.

7. Take your pumpkin cake out of the refrigerator and either use a palette knife to spread the buttercream over the cake or put it in a piping bag (or freezer bag with the corner snipped off) and pipe it on. I find piping ensures a more even layer. Use a palette knife to make it even and create the contours of a real pumpkin. Refrigerate to set and then you can use a warm spoon (dip a metal spoon in boiling water) to smooth out any rougher areas.

8. To make the stalk, shape green and brown sugar paste into a cone. Roll out the sugar paste and cut leaves from it and make tendrils. Work quickly while the sugar paste is soft and then leave in position to air dry and harden. I placed a layer of green and a layer of brown on top of one another and then twisted them together to create a two-tone autumn effect, but do whatever works for you as there is no right or wrong, only what makes you happy. Sprinkle a little edible glitter on the leaves to make it even more magical. This Bundt will keep for up to 5 days in an airtight container.

*Mini pumpkins variation: use this recipe to make mini pumpkins using a 12-hole Bundtlette® pan and add a cinnamon stick to the centre of each.*

# Pumpkin Bundt with Salted Caramel Frosting & Cinnamon Ice Cream

We don't have Thanksgiving in England but if we did this would be on the menu. I think Thanksgiving has such a wonderful sentiment of gratitude without the distraction and stress of finding everyone the perfect gift, which also allows the focus to be shifted onto the food which would, of course, make it by far my favourite holiday!

SERVES 12

**For the 12-cup Anniversary Bundt® pan:**
15g (1 tbsp/ ½oz) butter
15g (1 tbsp/ ½oz) plain flour

**For the cake:**
375g (1 ½ cups/3 sticks/13oz) unsalted butter, softened
500g (2 ½ cups/1lb 2oz) caster sugar
6 eggs
2 tsp vanilla bean paste
A pinch of salt
325g (1 ½ cups/11 ½oz) pumpkin purée
1 tsp ground cinnamon
1 tsp ground ginger
1 tsp mixed spice
¼ tsp ground nutmeg
400g (3 cups/14oz) self-raising flour

**For the frosting:**
60g (½ stick/2 ¼oz) unsalted butter
85g (½ cup/3oz) soft dark brown sugar
85ml (⅔ cup/5 ½ tbsp) double cream
A pinch of sea salt
125g (1 cup/4 ½oz) icing sugar

1. Preheat your oven to 160°C fan/180°C/350°F/gas 4.

2. Melt the butter, then use a pastry brush to brush it generously over the inside of a 12-cup Anniversary Bundt® pan, being careful to get into every nook and cranny. I find it easier to brush from the base up to prevent any butter pooling. Sift over the flour, moving the pan from side to side to coat it evenly, then tap it while inverted to remove any excess flour. Set aside until ready to use.

3. Cream the butter and sugar together until pale and fluffy. Add the eggs, mix well, then add the vanilla, salt, pumpkin purée and spices. Mix well until even. Sift over the flour, mix again and pour into the prepared pan. Bake for 1 hour or until a skewer inserted into the cake comes out clean. Leave to cool in the pan for 15 minutes before turning out onto a wire rack to cool completely.

4. To make the frosting, add the butter, sugar, cream and salt to a small saucepan and bring to the boil. Remove from the heat and leave to cool for 10 minutes. Tip in the icing sugar and mix until smooth. Pour over the Bundt, decorate with pecans and add a large red bow, if you wish.

5. When the ice cream is soft, stir through the cinnamon and then re-freeze. Scoop into the centre of the Bundt to serve. This Bundt will keep for up to 5 days in an airtight container.

**To decorate:**
100g (¾ cup + 2 tbsp/3 ½oz) pecans
A red ribbon (optional)

**To serve:**
500ml (18fl oz) tub of vanilla ice cream, softened
1 tbsp ground cinnamon

# Ginger & Chocolate Gingerbread House Bundt

———

This is like a Christmas ginger chocolate except you get a fabulous slice of it!

SERVES 8

**For the 9-cup Gingerbread House Bundt® pan:**

15g (1 tbsp/ ½oz) butter
15g (1 tbsp/ ½oz) plain flour

**For the cake:**

325g (3 sticks/11 ½oz) unsalted butter, softened
275g (1 ½ cups/9¾oz) golden caster sugar
100g (½ cup/3 ½oz) light muscovado sugar
4 eggs
1 tsp vanilla bean paste
2 tsp ground ginger
1 tsp sea salt
350g (2¾ cups/12oz) self-raising flour
170g (1 cup/6oz) dark chocolate chips
100g (1 cup/3 ½oz) preserved ginger, grated

**To decorate:**

4 tbsp icing sugar, for dusting

1. Preheat your oven to 160°C fan/180°C/350°F/gas 4.

2. Melt the butter, then use a pastry brush to brush it generously over the inside of a 9-cup Gingerbread House Bundt® pan, being careful to get into every nook and cranny. I find it easier to brush from the base up to prevent any butter pooling. Scatter over the flour, moving the pan from side to side to coat it evenly, then tap it while inverted to remove any excess flour. Set aside until ready to use.

3. Cream the butter and sugars together in a large mixing bowl and then add the eggs and vanilla and beat until smooth. Pour in the ginger, salt and flour and fold them in until just combined. Stir through the chocolate chips and grated ginger, then spoon the batter into the prepared pan. Bake for 45–50 minutes or until a skewer inserted into the cake comes out clean. Leave to cool in the pan for 15 minutes, then carefully invert onto a wire rack to cool completely.

4. Dust simply with a heavy snowfall of icing sugar and Christmas is served. Or alternatively make a thick paste by adding a little water to the icing sugar and pipe outlines for a roof and windows and other details. This Bundt will keep for several days.

# Chocolate & Cinnamon Christmas Tree Bundt with Cinnamon Buttercream & Marzipan Pine Cones

I'm not going to deceive you, this Bundt is a tiny bit fiddly but Christmas is all about detail and magical surprises, so imagine the delight of a slice of cake with a chocolate Christmas tree within it! It never ceases to impress all ages in my house and makes a thoughtful gift.

SERVES 10

**For the chocolate Christmas trees:**
25g (2 tbsp/1oz) cocoa powder
125g (¾ cup/4½oz) self-raising flour
125g (½ cup/4½oz) golden caster sugar
A pinch of salt
125g (1 stick + 1 tbsp/4½oz) unsalted butter, melted
2 eggs
1 tsp vanilla bean paste

**For the 12-cup Anniversary Bundt® pan**
15g (1 tbsp/½oz) butter
15g (1 tbsp/½oz) plain flour

1. Preheat your oven to 160°C fan/180°C/350°F/gas 4 and line a baking tray with a piece of baking parchment.

2. To make the Christmas trees, take a large mixing bowl and add the cocoa powder, flour, sugar and salt. Pour over the melted butter, eggs and vanilla and mix until smooth. Pour it into the baking tray and bake for 25 minutes or until a skewer inserted into the centre comes out clean. Remove from the oven and leave to cool completely. Once cool, use a small Christmas-tree-shaped cookie cutter (it needs to be relatively small so that it will fit within the width of the Bundt® pan) and cut Christmas trees from the chocolate sponge. Put the Christmas trees in the freezer while you make the batter for the Bundt.

3. To prepare the Bundt® pan, melt the butter, then use a pastry brush to brush it generously over the inside of a 12-cup Anniversary Bundt® pan, being careful to get into every nook and cranny. I find it easier to brush from the base up to prevent any butter pooling. Scatter over the flour, moving the pan from side to side to coat it evenly, then tap it while inverted to remove any excess flour. Set aside until ready to use.

**For the bundt:**
300g (2 ½ sticks/10 ½ oz)
   unsalted butter
200g (1 cup/7oz) caster sugar
4 eggs
1 tsp vanilla bean paste
75ml (⅓ cup/2 ½ fl oz)
   buttermilk
200g (1 ¼ cups/7oz) self-
   raising flour
½ tsp baking powder
½ tsp bicarbonate of soda
A pinch of salt
1 tsp ground cinnamon

**For the frosting:**
250g (2 sticks + 2 tbsp/9oz)
   unsalted butter
1 tbsp ground cinnamon
500g (4 ½ cups/1lb 2oz)
   icing sugar
50g (¼ cup/1 ¾ oz) white
   chocolate, melted

**To decorate:**
100g (1 cup/3 ½ oz) marzipan
50g (½ cup/1 ¾ oz) flaked
   almonds
Sprigs of rosemary
Icing sugar, for dusting

4. Cream together the butter and sugar in a large bowl. Add the eggs, vanilla and buttermilk and continue to beat until fully incorporated. Pour over the flour, baking powder, bicarbonate of soda, salt and cinnamon and beat until just combined. Pour half the mixture into the prepared pan. Take the Christmas trees out of the freezer and arrange them upside down in a row all around the Bundt ring, with as few spaces in between them as possible. Pour the remaining batter over the Christmas trees and then bake for 45–50 minutes or until a skewer inserted into the cake comes out clean. Leave to cool in the pan for 15 minutes, then invert onto a wire rack to cool completely.

5. To make the cinnamon frosting, beat the butter, cinnamon, icing sugar and melted white chocolate together until smooth. Spread over the Bundt.

6. To make the pine cones, shape a cone from the marzipan and then stick the pieces of flaked almond into it. Place on top of the Bundt, along with a few sprigs of rosemary and dust everything with snow, I mean icing sugar.

Image overleaf →

# Chocolate Christmas Pudding Bundt

———

This is a classic Christmas pudding's naughty little sister, who doesn't play by the rules. Filled with chocolate chunks and cocoa it will appeal to those who don't usually venture into the land of Christmas pudding. It can be kept for up to six weeks and 'fed' with more brandy, but it also tastes divine the day it's baked, so is very forgiving if you've run out of time. You can also buy ready-soaked fruit to save time.

SERVES 12

**For the soaked fruit :**
300ml (1 ¼ cups/ 10 ½ fl oz) brandy
200g (1 cup/ 7oz) currants
200g (1 cup/ 7oz) raisins
200g (1 cup/ 7oz) sultanas
200g (1 cup/ 7oz) mixed peel
50g (¼ cup/ 1 ¾ oz) glacé cherries

**For the 12-cup Bundt® pan:**
15g (1 tbsp/ ½ oz) butter
15g (1 tbsp/ ½ oz) cocoa powder

1. Add the brandy, currants, raisins, sultanas, mixed peel and cherries to a bowl and leave to soak overnight.

2. The next day, preheat your oven to 160°C fan/180°C/350°F/ gas 4. Melt the butter and then use a pastry brush to brush it generously over the inside of a 12-cup Bundt® pan, being careful to get into every nook and cranny. I find it easier to brush from the base up to prevent any butter pooling. Scatter over the cocoa powder, moving the pan from side to side to coat it evenly, then tap it while inverted to remove any excess cocoa. Set aside until ready to use.

3. Cream the butter and sugar together, add the eggs, beat them in and then add the spices and orange juice, mixing well. Pour in the soaked fruit and brandy and mix to combine. Mix the boiling water and cocoa together to make a paste and add it to the batter, followed by the grated marzipan, almonds, flour and chocolate chunks. Mix to combine and pour into the prepared pan. Cover the top with 2 layers of foil, pressing them securely to the pan, then place the pan in a roasting tray. Place the tray in the oven and pour boiling water around the Bundt in the roasting tray so it comes a couple of centimetres up the sides. Bake for 2 hours.

**For the cake:**
125g (1 stick + 1 tbsp/4½oz)
   unsalted butter
225g (1 cup/8oz) light
   muscovado sugar
2 eggs
1 tsp ground cinnamon
1 tsp ground ginger
1 tsp ground mixed spice
Juice of 1 orange
100ml (½ cup/3½fl oz) boiling
   water
100g (1 cup/3½oz) cocoa
   powder
100g (1 cup/3½oz) marzipan,
   grated
100g (¾ cup/3½oz) blanched
   almonds, chopped
200g (1¼ cups/7oz) plain flour
100g (½ cup/3½oz) dark
   chocolate, cut into chunks

**To serve:**
Brandy
Brandy butter
Holly leaves

4. Leave to cool in the pan. This will keep for weeks so you can add a splash of brandy every week in the build up to Christmas. Keep securely covered with foil and wrapped in a tea towel somewhere dark and cool. If you don't have time to let it soak for 6 weeks, it will still taste delicious even if you eat it on the same day it's made.

5. To serve, place your Bundt® pan in a roasting tray. Fill the tray with boiling water and cook at 160°C fan/180°C/350°F/gas 4, to heat through, for 1 hour. Leave to cool in the pan for 10 minutes, then invert onto a serving plate. Pour brandy over the pudding, turn out the lights and light it up! Serve with brandy butter and holly leaves for decoration.

# Chocolate & Caramel Layer Bundt with Milk Chocolate Hazelnut Ganache

---

A decadent chocolate Bundt with layers of the gooiest caramel, but the real star of this show is the ganache. The milk chocolate ganache has chopped and roasted hazelnuts stirred through it and sets with a joyful shine. If you don't have time to make the caramel, you can use a shop-bought one instead.

SERVES 12

**For the 12-cup Anniversary Bundt pan:**
15g (1 tbsp/ ½oz) butter
15g (1 tbsp/ ½oz) cocoa powder

**For the cake:**
75g (²/₃ cup/2¾oz) cocoa powder
135g (1 cup/4¾oz) soft light brown sugar
175g (1 cup/6oz) golden caster sugar
65g (½ stick/2¼oz) unsalted butter, melted
1 tsp vanilla bean paste
235ml (1cup/8 ¼ oz) boiling water
2 eggs
175ml (1 cup/6fl oz) buttermilk
200g (1 ½ cups/7oz) self-raising flour
½ tsp baking powder
½ tsp bicarbonate of soda

1. Preheat your oven to 160°C fan/180°C/350°F/gas 4.

2. Melt the butter, then use a pastry brush to brush it generously over the inside of a 12-cup Anniversary Bundt® pan, being careful to get into every nook and cranny. I find it easier to brush from the base up to prevent any butter pooling. Sift over the cocoa powder, moving the pan from side to side to coat it evenly, then tap it while inverted to remove any excess cocoa. Set aside until ready to use.

3. Take a large mixing bowl and add the cocoa powder, sugars, butter and vanilla. Pour over the boiling water and use a whisk to mix everything together until smooth. Whisk the eggs and buttermilk together in a small bowl, then mix them into the chocolate mixture. Fold through the flour, baking powder and bicarbonate of soda. Pour the batter into the prepared pan and bake for 50–55 minutes. Leave to cool in the pan for 15 minutes, then invert onto a wire rack to cool completely.

4. To make the caramel, add the sugar and water to a heavy-based pan. Cook gently at first to dissolve the sugar, then increase the heat and, without stirring, wait for it to turn a deep, golden amber. It shouldn't be mahogany, more of a gingery burnt orange. If you get a pocket of mahogany amber, simply swirl the pan. Take the pan off the heat and pour in the double cream (it won't splutter as it would if you added water), whisk vigorously and then add the butter, it will melt in a few minutes. Whisk until evenly coloured, sprinkle over the salt, then pour into a clean bowl to cool and set until ready to assemble.

**For the caramel:**

250g (1 ½ cups/9oz) caster
   sugar
90ml (6 tbsp/3fl oz) water
125ml (½ cup/4fl oz) double
   cream
110g (1 stick/3¾oz) unsalted
   butter
1 tsp salt

**For the hazelnut ganache:**

150g (¾ cup + 1 tbsp/5½oz)
   milk chocolate
200ml (¾ cup + 2 tbsp/7fl oz)
   double cream
50g (⅓ cup/1¾oz) hazelnuts,
   roasted and finely chopped
   (you can buy them ready
   roasted and chopped)

**To decorate:**

Gold-foil-wrapped chocolates
Whipped cream
Sparklers

5. To assemble the Bundt, carefully slice horizontally into 3 layers. Spread the caramel between them and sandwich the layers back together. Set aside.

6. For the ganache, break up the chocolate and place it in a heatproof bowl with the cream and microwave to melt them together. Whisk with a small whisk or fork until even. Pour in the chopped hazelnuts and stir them through. Place the Bundt on a wire rack with a plate beneath it. Pour the ganache over the entire Bundt, re-using any ganache that's fallen onto the plate below, so that the entire Bundt is covered. Leave to set.

7. Serve with the centre filled with gold-foil-wrapped chocolates piled high, a dollop of whipped cream and a few sparklers to bring in a gold and sparkly New Year. This Bundt will keep for a few days in an airtight container.

Image overleaf →

# Homemade Cake Release

————

I discovered this because I ran out of cake release spray. It really does work but unlike bought spray you have to brush it on. I find a bullet blender gets the finest results and so it gets into all the nooks and crannies of the pan more easily. It's also a game changer in that it's better for the planet and you know exactly what the ingredients are (plus it's much kinder on your wallet than cake release spray).

MAKES ENOUGH TO
GENEROUSLY COAT
AROUND 20 TINS

200g (1½ cups/7oz) plain flour
200ml (1 cup/7fl oz)
    vegetable oil
200g (1 cup + 1 tbsp/7oz)
    shortening

1. Put all the ingredients into a blender or bullet blender and process until smooth. Store in a jar in your refrigerator. It will keep for 3 months.

2. To use, simply brush into the Bundt® pan. Never be caught out again!

# Index

Note: page numbers in **bold** refer to illustrations.

# Conversion chart

| TSP | TBSP | FL OZ | CUP |
|-----|------|-------|-----|
| 3 | 1 | ½ | 1/16 |
| 6 | 2 | 1 | ⅛ |
| 12 | 4 | 2 | ¼ |
| 18 | 6 | 3 | ⅜ |
| 24 | 8 | 4 | ½ |
| 36 | 12 | 6 | ¾ |
| 48 | 16 | 8 | 1 |
| 96 | 32 | 16 | 2 |

| ML | TSP | TBSP | CUP | OZ |
|-----|-----|------|-----|-----|
| 2.5 | ½ | | | |
| 5 | 1 | ⅓ | | |
| 15 | 3 | 1 | | |
| 60 | 12 | 4 | ¼ | 2 |
| 115 | | 7 ½ | | 4 |
| 120 | | 8 | ½ | |
| 150 | | 10 | | 6 |
| 160 | | 11 | ⅔ | |
| 180 | | 12 | ¾ | |
| 230 | | 15 ½ | | 8 |
| 240 | | 16 | 1 | |
| 285 | | 19 | | 10 |
| 340 | | 23 | 1 ½ | 12 |

# About the Author

**Melanie Johnson** is a chef and food writer. She was born in Australia, raised between the Austrian mountains and the British countryside, and is now based in London where she lives with her daughter, Lilybee, and their beloved cockapoos, Elsa and Arthur.

She is a Leith's trained chef and host of London supper clubs and cookery classes.

Melanie is the food columnist at *Country Life* magazine where she has been sharing her recipes in her *Kitchen Garden Cook* column every week for almost a decade.

*Bundt* is Melanie's first book and you can find her @melathomeltd and www.melathome.com

# Thank you

To my beautiful daughter Lilybee, for waiting patiently as I baked a million Bundts – I love you.

To my parents, Heidi and Malcolm, my sister and her husband, Sam and Symon, my brother, Alex, and all of my nieces, Bella, Alessara, India and Jade for listening as I bored them with questions about Bundts and also for eating an 'abundtance' of them as I recipe tested (the nieces firmly knew the banana and chocolate Bundt was vastly better with even more chocolate). I love you all so much and will never forget such love and kindness in the build up to writing this book when I was fighting breast cancer.

To my publisher, Elizabeth Bond and also Fionn Hargreaves at Ebury, it has been a privilege and joy to work with you and watch my little book idea come to life, that you very generously renamed a 'big' book idea.

To my agent Becca Barr for being the most wonderful, diligent and patient agent with all things professional and yet a true friend for everything else in between.

To Pauline Clements at Nordic Ware for providing an array of beautiful bakeware to create everything you see in this book!

To Nassima Rothaker for her photographs and Bella Haycraft Mee and Jodie Nixon who helped bake with enthusiasm and passion to make this dream come true.